I HATE MYSELFIE

I HATE MYSELFIE

a collection of essays by

SHANE DAWSON

Keywords PRESS

ATRIA PAPERBACK

New York • London • Toronto • Sydney • New Delhi

ATRIA PAPERBACK

An Imprint of Simon & Schuster, Inc.
1230 Avenue of the Americas
New York, NY 10020

First Keywords Press/**ATRIA** PAPERBACK edition March 2015

Keywords Press/**ATRIA** PAPERBACK colophon are trademarks of
Simon & Schuster, Inc.

For information about special discounts for bulk purchases,
please contact Simon & Schuster Special Sales at 1-866-506-1949
or business@simonandschuster.com.

The Simon & Schuster Speakers Bureau can bring authors to your
live event. For more information or to book an event contact the
Simon & Schuster Speakers Bureau at 1-866-248-3049 or visit our
website at www.simonspeakers.com.

Interior design by Dana Sloan

Manufactured in the United States of America

10 9 8 7 6 5 4

Library of Congress Cataloging-in-Publication Data has been
applied for.

ISBN 978-1-4767-9154-8
ISBN 978-1-4767-9158-6 (ebook)

This book is dedicated to my hilarious and caring mother. Thank you for giving me so much unconditional love and fuck you for giving me your fat arms and wonky eye.

CONTENTS

ABOUT THE ART

I have a lot of really talented fans. So I thought it would be fun to ask some of them to create pictures inspired by the essays. I sent each of them an excerpt and asked him or her to draw whatever they felt like. As you'll see, the results are sometimes amazing, sometimes hilarious, and always unflattering, considering I have a VERY hard face to draw.

I HATE MYSELFIE: AN INTRODUCTION

ABOUT THE ARTIST

Isabella Piccione is currently a freshman in high school and has had a passion for art for as long as she can remember. She lives in Connecticut, and you can follow her on Twitter at @stylesftdawson.

Hi. I'm Shane Dawson. Some of you might know me from my videos on the internet. Some of you might know me from the movie I directed entitled *Not Cool.* And some of you might know me as the guy you saw on the cover of this book who has an incredibly punchable face. I'm all of those things and more! I also have an incredibly punchable body, but none of you will ever get to see that.

For the record, I don't really hate myself, but I do hate the way I portray myself online. Hence, "myselfie." See what I did there? Online I'm this loud, outrageous, confident guy who acts like nothing bothers him and he has the whole world at his fingertips. In reality, I'm a shy, quiet guy who would rather spend his nights lying in bed watching Netflix than being a valuable member of society. If I could spend my entire life underneath a heating blanket with a handful of my own balls I would happily do so.

I'm not saying that I don't like the stuff I put out into the world, because I genuinely enjoy my videos and think they are funny. What I'm saying is that I embrace the fact that I have a punchable face, and that if I could punch myself without feeling it I would. Sometimes I scroll through my Instagram page and audibly groan. What is the point of posting four pictures a day of yourself doing the same duck face in four different locations? If you go through my Instagram feed it's like a flip book of me thinking I'm WAY more attractive than I am. It's nauseating. But feel free to follow me at @SHANEDAWSON! You can also follow me on Twitter, where I post important tweets like: "I think I just pooped blood. Should I go to the doctor? Nvmd, just gonna google it," and "Ugh. Is Emma Stone still a thing? Can that be over yet?" It gets really deep. I'm a social warrior, clearly.

In this book, you'll get to see the real me, not the "me" you see on YouTube. You will get to know what's really in my head, and I'm warning you it's not pretty. It's a twisted land of self-hatred, sadness, and lots of repressed anger toward every person who's ever hurt me. ENJOY! Don't worry, I threw in some dick and fart jokes to make the stories a little easier to handle. Kind of like mixing in some peanut butter with your medicine, which by the way my mom used to do. You haven't lived till you've had a Vicodin peanut butter marshmallow fluff sandwich. I can still taste the numbing of my emotions. Delicious.

I urge you to sit back, enjoy, and know that in the end things have gotten better for me. And they will for you too, if that's anything you're worried about. Feel free to laugh at my misfortune and get that feeling of "Wow, my life is SO much better than THAT guy's."

Obviously joking but semi-serious,
Shane Dawson

MY DESTINEE

ABOUT THE ARTIST

Anna Siefken has been drawing her entire life, but it wasn't until an art class in the sixth grade that she decided to start taking it seriously. She currently resides in Norwalk, Connecticut, and, at just fifteen years old, spends her days drawing, designing shirts, and making YouTube videos. You can find some of her designs at pistachiothegreat.spreadshirt.com.

Nothing gives me more anxiety than getting a haircut. Just the thought of going to a salon—I mean barber—and having a stranger touch my head while asking me personal questions about my life makes my nerves shoot through the roof. It's the same feeling a wicker chair gets when a circa-2006 Kelly Clarkson takes a seat. TENSE. But sometimes you have to bite the bullet and let Kelly Clarkson sit on your face. The day after my high school graduation was one of those times. I had rocked the same shoulder-length frizzy do since I was twelve years old, and the style had run its course. There was only so much I could do with it. Actually there were only three things I could do with it: wash it, let it air-dry, and pray to God I didn't get lice. My hair was lice's dream habitat. The amount of poof and waves made it practically a tropical getaway for those little fuckers. I'm sure every time I walked by a homeless dude his lice would only WISH they were having an adventure in my twisted, knotted labyrinth of a hairdo. I might not have had girls double-taking when I walked by, but damn it, the lice wanted a motherfucking piece.

So one hot Monday afternoon in June of 2006 I pulled into a shopping center parking lot and stared at the SUPERCUTS sign that was casting a shadow on my car. This was the day. I had prepared myself for this moment for weeks, and I was ready. I took a deep breath, took a bite of a protein cookie—which, let's face it, was just a cookie—and stumbled through the door with fear in my eyes. The woman at the register looked up at me with a welcoming smile and asked what she could do for me. I asked for a haircut. She paused. Awkward silence. Then she said, "Women or men's?" Yep. It was definitely time for a haircut. She walked me over to the station and I looked around, scoping out what the situation was. The situation was pretty clear: these people had NO fucking idea what they were doing and it smelled like El Pollo Loco had farted and locked the doors for two weeks. I was too lazy to find another salon—I mean barber—so I just sat in a stained purple swivel chair and awaited my fate.

Receptionist: Destinee will be with you soon. She's in the back talking to her ex-husband on the phone.
Me: Definitely didn't need all that information, but thank you.

So I sat and flipped through a Spanish version of *People* magazine from fifteen years ago, thinking, "Wow, I don't know who this Selena chick is but she is DEFINITELY going places!" As I skimmed through the magazine my Razr phone started vibrating and playing Ashlee Simpson's "Pieces of Me." It was my mom calling.

Me: Hey, Mom.
Mom: Did you do it yet?!
Me: No. Still waiting. I think my stylist is in the middle of a custody battle right now.

Mom: Oh! Fun! Are you excited?!

Me: Not really. I'm scared she's gonna make me look like a troll doll.

Mom: Awwwww, but you're MY little troll doll!

Me: Not really the response I was looking for, but thanks, Mom.

Mom: Well, call me when you're done! And email me a picture on your pager!

Me: That makes no sense.

Mom: Love you!

As I reached for another decade-old magazine my "stylist" walked up to greet me. I put "stylist" in quotes because her cosmetology certificate looked like it was printed on the back of a Denny's placemat. My expectations for this haircut were about the same as when I walk into an Eddie Murphy movie. I know it's going to be bad, but maybe it will give people a few laughs. I like to spread joy even if it's at my expense.

I looked her up and down, and my expectations went from an Eddie Murphy movie to any Adam Sandler film made after 2008. This situation was *Grown Ups* bad. It looked like she had cut her hair without scissors and had instead chosen to cover her head in peanut butter and raw meat and hang upside down from a tree branch in a dog park. She was wearing one of those shitty Halloween shirts that said "This IS my costume." Did I mention it was June? She had hoop earrings so big I could have hanged myself with them, which I thought would come in handy if the haircut went as horribly as I suspected it would.

She took a sip of the world's biggest Starbucks Frappuccino and let out a small uncontainable burp. This was going great.

> Destinee: So, what do you want?
> Me: For you to tell me that you are just another sassy front-desk person and Destinee is still in the back screaming at her baby daddy?
> Destinee: Nope. I'm your Destinee.
> Me: That pun is particularly terrifying. I'm going to use the restroom. I'll be right back.

At that moment I wished I was in a horror film, because "I'll be right back" usually means you aren't going to be back, you're going to die. I wished I was dead. Now, I know what you're thinking: why didn't I just leave? Because I have a syndrome called No Balls Disorder, that's why. Basically I have no fucking balls and I say yes to everything to avoid conflict. I've gotten better at it with age but at this time I was eighteen and terrified of everything and everyone around me. Including wicker furniture.

I went into the bathroom and locked the door. I stood in front of the mirror and looked at myself. I tried to make myself see something that wasn't there: a great hairstyle. Maybe if I could convince myself that my hair looked ok the way it was I could just get out of there and never get a haircut ever again? Ya, that seemed doable. I took out my phone and started taking hundreds of selfies. Different angles, different faces, lots of filters. I was trying my hardest to find at least one picture where I felt like I didn't look completely unattractive. It didn't happen. It made it worse. After the bathroom photo shoot I decided it was time to go back out there and face my Destinee.

Me: I need help. I'm scared. Can you please make me look like less of a lesbian?

Destinee: Awww, don't be so down on yourself. And people shouldn't judge you by your hair or by your lifestyle.

She thought I was a woman. Perfect. At this point I wanted to just shave my fucking head.

Me: Can you just make me look like a guy?

Destinee: Any specific guy? Did you look through my magazines?

Me: I don't really think I can pull off Enrique Iglesias from ten years ago, so maybe just make me look like Brad Pitt?

Silence. Challenge not accepted. Out of the realm of possibility.

Me: Ok . . . how about Jay Leno?

Destinee: Jay Leno? Nobody wants to fuck Jay Leno.

Me: My grandmother strongly disagrees, but ok, noted.

Destinee: Just trust me. I'm gonna just do my thing.

Judging from her personal style and the zero customers in line for her, I couldn't imagine her "thing" being revolutionary, but she was my only hope. She grabbed the scissors, then looked at my head for a moment, put the scissors back down, and replaced them with the biggest set of electric clippers I've ever seen. This wasn't a job for flimsy pieces of metal; this was a job for something that could mow a lawn. I avoided looking at the mirror because I didn't want to see the damage being done. Similar to how when I eat at a restaurant I keep my eyes clear of any reflective surface. I looked down at my lap and saw chunks of hair gathering near my crotch. The amount of nappy dandruff-sprinkled hair that was falling from my head made it look like God was shaving his ancient pubes. It was of biblical proportions. I then heard something that you never want to hear a hairstylist mutter.

Destinee: Oops.

Oops?! OOPS?! You better have spilled some of your Starbucks fattaccino on my smock because if that "oops" is in any way related to my haircut I WILL ONE-STAR-YELP YOU SO HARD YOU'LL HAVE TO CHANGE YOUR FUCKING NAME AND MOVE TO CANADA! (Yelp wasn't really a thing back then but hey, you get the point.)

Destinee: I think I took a little too much off the back. I might have to even it out. Are you ok with that?

Am I OK WITH THAT?! ARE YOU FUCKING KIDDING ME, YOU BARELY GED-ACHIEVING, TACKY-DRESSED SNAGGLE-TOOTHED CUNT?! NO! This was NOT ok!

Me: Sure.

Once again, No Balls Disorder. Like any girl having sex with Hugh Hefner, I just closed my eyes and waited for it to be over. I heard the sound of the clippers turning off and a loud sigh come from the disaster behind me. It was time to see what my head looked like. I opened my eyes and what I saw wasn't a haircut, it was a hair MASSACRE. It was bed head if I slept on a bed of starving rats. It was so short I could see my eyebrows, and NOBODY wants to see that.

Me: It's . . . short.
Destinee: Ya. But it looks super . . . umm . . . sexy?

I still can't believe she said that without thurping.

Destinee: You know . . . there is a way to make it look longer.
Me: Nah, I've gotten that email before. Trust me, it's a scam.
Destinee: We could always straighten it.

Straighten it? What does that mean? How does one . . . straighten? Like one of those creepy Christian camps that weirdo parents send their gay kids to?

Me: What do you mean?

She whipped out a large phallic object and turned it on "extra high."

Destinee: I'll show you.

I wish books could have movie montages, because the next twenty minutes were straight out of a nineties Freddie Prinze Jr. movie. I was the ugly girl and Destinee was my slutty sister giving me a makeover. I was going from "ugly" to "not as ugly if you squint your eyes a little." It was a dream come true. After lots of clamping, straightening, and the scent of burned hair, she was done. I looked in the mirror and I actually didn't look THAT terrible! It was a miracle!

Little did she know she'd created a monster. From that day forward I've never met a straightener I didn't DESTROY with my nappy-ass hair. If it were possible to marry a straightener I would. I would figure out a way to consummate that marriage. It would be super gross and slightly dangerous but I would do it.

I went to my car and breathed a huge sigh of relief. I looked at myself in the rearview mirror and stared at the new me. I wasn't the prettiest girl at the prom but I was definitely good enough to get date raped.

BING.

My mom texted me asking for a picture of my new look. I opened up my camera and took a picture. I looked at it and shockingly, I was happy with it. I didn't have to take a thousand, I didn't have to get fifty different angles, I didn't even need a filter. I was happy with it the way it was, for the first time in a long time. Click.

SENT.

MY HIGH SCHOOL MUSICAL

Michelle
Mendes

ABOUT THE ARTIST

Michelle Mendes is an eighteen-year-old artist from the land Down Under—Australia! She has loved to draw ever since she was old enough to hold a pencil. Her skills have expanded over the years, ranging from all different styles of media and art. You can follow her on Twitter at @Michelle25696 and on Instagram at @MICHELLE25696.

Lots of high schools are known for something. Football, sex scandals, shootings, or, more often than not, a yearly musical. My school wasn't known for anything besides having a principal who died while eating a hot dog. We weren't very good at anything in particular. Nothing set us apart from the rival schools and we were usually parents' second choice on where to send their kids. The school three miles down the road was famous for a multitude of things. They had a killer football team, and they had no sexual predators on staff. Mary-Kate and Ashley even filmed episodes for one of their shows there a few years back. Analogy: if the school district had been the parent, then that school would have been the golden child and we would have been the child with one leg longer than the other. But that didn't stop us from trying!

Every year our school would put on a disaster known as the spring musical. It was chock-full of bad acting, nervous on-stage vomiting, and some sort of love triangle between a girl and two guys. But usually the girl was thrown to the side, if you catch my drift. It was a yearly event that I stayed as far away from as I could. Until my senior year.

I was one of those kids who would do whatever my friends wanted even if I knew it was wrong. The number of times we went through a Del Taco drive-through and acted like we had Tourette's syndrome was countless. The leader of my group was a girl named Tara. She was a fun, loud free spirit with more sexual experience than most of the teachers. And that's a fact. There was a rumor that she gave one of our teachers the clap. She was everything I wanted to be (minus the clap part). She wasn't afraid to take fashion risks or hit on strangers. Life was her chem lab, and she was constantly experimenting, whereas I was stuck in remedial math class adding up the consequences of any risk I could take. One day she came up to me with an idea I knew was bad from the second it left her dick-suckin' lips.

Tara: We should try out for the musical!

Me: What? Why? Can't we just pretend we have Tourette's and go through the Burger King drive-through again?

Tara: We did that yesterday. Come on! It'll be fun!

Me: That's what you said about searching through my mom's closet. And finding that Polaroid of her crawling on my dad's naked legs was the opposite of fun.

Tara: Don't you trust me?

No. I did not trust her. For good reason! This is the same girl who thought it was a good idea to watch water-birth videos on YouTube while we were eating Thai food. But because I go along with everybody my answer was obvious.

Me: Yes.

So that day Tara and I went to the auditions, which were being held in the chorus room. As we walked in she started pointing out our competition.

Tara: That's Lacy Barnes. Good at high notes. Bad at suckin' dick.

Me: How do you know that?

Tara: I fucked her boyfriend a few times. Nothing serious though. Just during lunch period.

Me: Right.

Tara: That's Jay Hernandez. Bad at high notes but REALLY good at suckin' dick. You gotta watch out for him. He ALWAYS gets the lead.

Me: Are you saying he sucks the teacher's dick?

Tara: NO! That's disgusting.

Pot. Kettle. Black. Continue.

Tara: But the teacher doesn't cast the play. The student teacher does.

Me: Student teacher?

Tara: Ya. It's this guy who graduated last year. I forgot his name but if he's coming back to his old high school he must not be getting any in college. Jay's gonna be on that dick like sprinkles on fro yo.

Me: Is it gay that my stomach just grumbled?

Tara: Oh my God. There she is. Patty Stevens.

Patty Stevens was every musical casting director's wet dream. She had long flowing blond hair, big doe eyes that caught the light perfectly, and a voice bigger than her ass (and her ass was pretty big). She always had a different boyfriend who would cling to her side like a personal assistant. Feeding her, giving her sips of her off-campus Frappuccino, and fixing her bangs when they got too scattered. There were lots of rumors about Patty floating around school. One was that she had super-rich parents who'd invented fake belly rings. Another was that she'd had four nose jobs and an abortion in the same semester. That last one was more of a compliment considering we were all jealous of her talent for multitasking. When Patty Stevens was auditioning for a musical, she was getting the lead. No question. The student teacher, Raul, walked in, and Tara was right. He looked hungry for his high school glory days and even hungrier for cock. I was doomed to get a spot in the back of the chorus.

Raul: Hello, everyone! It's SO good to be back in my old home! I missed this SO much! Jay, you better get your booty out of my old desk, you silly bitch!

Yep. Jay was going to get the lead for sure. And possibly bent over a desk.

Raul: Let's get these auditions started! Who's first?!

The auditions went by extremely slowly. For every amazing performance there were about six horrendous ones that deserved to end with stone throwing and a possible guillotine situation. Then it was my turn, and I was horrified. I didn't know we were going to have to sing that day so I didn't have a song prepared. So I performed something by heart, something that, if done right, was sure to bring out some tears in the audience.

> Me: Hi. My name is Shane and I'm going to be singing "A Moment Like This" by American Idol winner Kelly Clarkson.

Let's just say I'm no Kelly Clarkson. After my horrible rendition I left the stage. Tara went after me. She sang some show tune I had never heard before. It wasn't bad. I was actually impressed. I was so proud that I forgot I'd tanked and started beaming for her. She sat back down and I grabbed her for a hug. There was a moment I thought she could actually get the lead . . . until I heard what came next.

> Patty: Hi! My name is Patty and I'm going to be singing "Somewhere over the Rainbow."

Shit. Not only did she blow it away, she actually cried while performing without missing a note. She was a true diva. She got a standing ovation from her peers and Raul couldn't contain himself. He squealed with pleasure like a sadistic pig getting branded by a hot iron. She was seriously born to be a leading lady; there was no questioning it.

The next day the results were posted on the door of the

chorus room after school. Just like in the movies, we all ran there after the bell rang to see what our parts were. There was screaming, crying, and lots of fake hugging. Tara and I made our way up to the door and took a deep breath.

Tara: You ready?
Me: As long as I'm not a tree I'll be happy.

We both looked and saw our fate. Tara was cast as the second lead, which was amazing! I was cast as "Fat Funny Tourist." "Fat" wasn't in the name but trust me, after reading the script, I knew it should have been. My only line was "WHO'S HUNGRY?!" and I was wearing a safari outfit that was "two sizes too small." Just like Patty, I was born for this role.

The next day we went to our first read-through. The cast was made up of a collection of many different types of people, but they were all nerds. There were the gay nerds, the book nerds, the chorus nerds, the drama nerds, and of course the lesbian nerds. Although the lesbian nerds weren't in the cast, technically. They were helping to build the sets and rig all the stage lighting. I for sure thought I wasn't going to fit in because I wasn't really a nerd. I was more of a loser. And trust me, there's a difference. I wasn't super smart or in possession of some kind of awesome skill. I was just a normal fat dude with sweat-gland issues.

The door opened and in walked a large woman with a look of menace smeared across her face. Everyone stopped talking and gave her their full attention. This was our director, Mrs. Welch. For the next two months, she would be the Ursula to my Little Mermaid.

> Mrs. Welch: Hello. I'm Mrs. Welch. I'm sure some of you have heard of me. If you haven't, you will. I don't take this job lightly. This musical will be perfect because it HAS to be. Anyone have a problem with that?

She was a true Disney villain. She had the face of a woman who killed puppies and ate them with a side of children's tears for dipping. She walked like a pirate with a wooden leg. She even had a belt made out of rope. Every year she would come to our school to direct the play and none of us knew what she did out in the real world. I'm guessing she owned a shooting range. I knew this wasn't going to be easy so I did what I knew how to do best. I tried to quit. I went to walk out the door but was stopped by her large-and-in-charge arm. There was a collection of spider veins on it that looked like a GPS map of Los Angeles during heavy traffic. So many BOLD DARK LINES.

> Mrs. Welch: Where do you think you're going?
>
> Me: I just remembered I can't do the musical because I have to do homework.
>
> Mrs. Welch: Did you audition?
>
> Me: Yes.
>
> Mrs. Welch: Did you get a part?

Me: Yes.

Mrs. Welch: Do you think it's fair to your other cast mates to leave them and force them to find a replacement? Do you think the president can just LEAVE the White House and let them FIGURE IT OUT?

Me: I'm playing Fat Tourist. That's hardly the president.

Mrs. Welch: Sit down.

Me: But—

Mrs. Welch: If you don't sit down I will make you sit down.

Me: You technically can't—

She flexed her big arm and the roads of Los Angeles EX-PANDED. I ran back to my chair in sheer terror.

A week later we started doing full rehearsals. We were on the auditorium stage working out our moves and our songs. In between songs we would sit backstage and hang out while Mrs. Welch took care of her IBS in the bathroom. Most of the conversations between the kids were way more sexual than I expected. I had no idea that nerds got laid so much! I heard at least three different stories about braces getting caught on pubes and two different stories about having sex with a pro-tractor. It was truly enlightening.

Patty never engaged in these conversations though. She would sit by herself and read over her lines. She had a way about her that made her seem better than everyone else but nobody was mad at her for that. Everyone felt that she really *was* better. It's probably similar to the way people treat Oprah. You just let her do her thing and don't bother her with your petty normal-people problems. I felt a connection with Patty, but I was too afraid to talk to her. There was something about her that was sad that I couldn't put my finger on. I knew that deep down underneath that perfect exterior something was broken and felt sure it was something that I could relate to. But instead of trying, I just left her alone. Until the big night.

It was opening night and our two months of hard work had finally paid off. We had rehearsed every day for four hours after school. Mrs. Welch might have been the devil in a suit made out of human skin, but she was incredibly talented at getting kids to seem semi-talented onstage. If you wore earplugs and squinted your eyes halfway shut, you might have thought you were watching a real show. The auditorium was filling up with paying customers and they were ready to be entertained! Backstage we were all freaking out with excitement while Mrs. Welch walked around inspecting our costumes.

> Mrs. Welch: Hike up those pants! Nobody wants to see your ass! Tuck in that shirt! Suck in that gut!

She made her rounds until she got to the end of the line, which was me in my small safari costume.

> Mrs. Welch: Shane! Are you wearing an undershirt?
> Me: Yes. My mom calls it my sweat catcher.
> Mrs. Welch: Go back behind that set and take it off! I want to see skin popping out between those stressed buttons!

Me: Ok.

Mrs. Welch: And if you see Patty tell her to get her pretty ass out here! We're five minutes away from show time!

I went behind the set and standing in the darkness was Patty. She was hunched over crying behind a fake door. Her shirt was only half-buttoned.

Me: Um . . . Patty?

Patty: Oh! Hey. I was just getting ready. Sorry. I'll be done in a minute.

Me: Are you ok?

Patty: Huh? Oh ya, I'm fine.

She sniffled and tried to play it off. But I knew something was up. Looking at her body, I knew exactly what her problem was. She wasn't fat by any means but she was soft, and the shirt she was trying to fit into wasn't the most flattering for her figure.

Me: Want me to ask wardrobe if they have a different shirt?

She looked me in the eyes and saw someone who really got her. What I saw was just a person, a person who needed help.

Patty: How bad does it look?

Me: Not bad at all.

Patty: I got nervous last night and ate my brother's entire

birthday cake. I feel so fat and nothing is fitting. Everyone is going to laugh at me. And everyone is taking pictures and video. I'm gonna look like a fat pig.

Me: You don't look fat. Especially next to me. If you want I can stand next to you during the cast photo. I can even eat a whole cake first. I skipped my after-lunch snack so I can probably take down a cake.

Patty: [laughs] You aren't nervous?

Me: No. Because I practiced a lot. And so did you. Even if you went out onstage and were the fattest person in the world it wouldn't matter, because when you open your mouth to sing it will shut the entire auditorium up. Everyone will forget about everything and only be able to focus on your voice. You are seriously the best singer I've ever heard. And I'm not just saying that.

Patty: Really?

Me: Ya. And hearing you say that you feel fat makes me really happy. 'Cause it means you aren't perfect. 'Cause damn it, it was getting really hard to not secretly hate you.

Patty: Thanks.

She finished getting ready. I took off my undershirt and got my costume back together.

Me: Now let's go out there and kick some ass.

She gave me a hug, and we walked out together ready to kill

it. The show was a success in some ways. Patty was amazing, Tara was great, and I totally nailed my "WHO'S HUNGRY?!" line. Of course there were some sour parts. Mainly when Mrs. Welch got wasted on cheap wine and yelled at people in the audience for not laughing at certain jokes or when Raul got caught making out with one of the lesbian set builders (didn't see that one coming). But even after all that it was still a night that I will always remember fondly. If you want to see pictures, just Google "Shane Dawson fat wearing safari hat 2006." You're welcome.

TWO FIRST KISSES

Sydney
Levine
IG-@_just_that_artsy_

ABOUT THE ARTIST

Sydney Levine *is fourteen years old and is a self-taught artist from Austin, Texas. She has been interested in art ever since she was a toddler, but she became truly motivated when she began sharing her work on the internet in the summer of 2013. Her favorite subjects to draw are animals, movie characters, and Shane Dawson. Follow her on Instagram at @_just_that_artsy.*

When I tell people my first relationship was when I was twenty-one they assume I grew up Amish. They also assume I'm an insanely repressed, closeted homosexual. Considering I'm only twenty-six, there's still plenty of time for me to explore my gay side. I can even picture myself at age fifty, getting my balls stepped on by a guy wearing a leather mask and screaming expletives in my face. The saddest part is that not only did I experience my first relationship at twenty-one, it was also the age when I had my first kiss. I swear I'm not Amish. The gay thing is questionable.

One night I was hanging out at a friend's house and she had a new roommate who was from Canada. I have an unhealthy obsession with Canada. I watch all their shows, I know all their catchphrases, and I try to incorporate "aboot" into my speech as often as possible. I don't know what got me so hooked on the maple people. Maybe it was the imaginary relationship I had with Avril Lavigne when I was thirteen? Or maybe it was the moment Jimmy got shot on *Degrassi*, which made me empathize with the whole country. Either way, I had maple syrup running through my veins, and not just because I used to drink Aunt Jemima out of the bottle.

When I met this new roommate I wanted to know everything about her. That's a lie. I wanted to know everything about her homeland and why they drank milk out of bags. We talked for hours and she educated me on everything I ever wanted to know about Canada. I learned why they like ketchup chips and why they are all so polite. She was like a real-life Wikipedia, and all I had to do was type in a question and she would pop out the answer. We hung out for the next week or so, and I don't think either of us was thinking it would be anything more than a friendship based on the mutual love of her homeland.

The third time we hung out I went over to her place to pick her up and she was crying in the parking lot with a suitcase. This was the beginning of the end of our friendship.

Me: What's wrong?

Canadian: I got kicked out of my apartment.

Me: What? Why??

Canadian: We got into a fight about something stupid and she kicked me out.

Me: Where are you going to go?

Canadian: I don't know. I'll have to find a place.

Me: Well . . . you can stay with me till you find one.

And that, my friends, was the dumbest idea I had ever had. Hey, girl that I just started hanging out with, wanna MOVE IN?! I didn't realize how insane it sounded because to me I just saw a friend in need, but at the age of twenty-one having a girl move into your small apartment isn't something sane people do. She reluctantly said yes because she really didn't have another option. That night we were lying in bed watching TV. I repeat: LYING IN BED WATCHING TV. Another not-so-bright idea when you are twenty-one and friends with a girl. Anyways, we were lying in bed watching TV and we started to cuddle. Now, this was the first time I had ever cuddled with a girl if you don't count my mom. My mom and I used to cuddle on the couch and watch shows about women getting brutally murdered, but that's another story. As we cuddled we both eyed each other with an "Are we doing this?" look. I'm not sure either of us was actually super interested in dating the other, but we were both lonely and sad so it just kind of happened. We decided not to kiss or do anything, mainly because we were nervous but also because we were halfway through an episode of *Hoarders* and we didn't want to miss the part where the guy found all the woman's dead cats.

The next morning we woke up and went to breakfast. It was the first time I had ever been to breakfast with a girl so I didn't know how to act. I assumed everybody in the restaurant thought we'd had sex that night and were there to replenish, but that wasn't the case. I didn't want people to think I did that, especially since at the time I was pretty religious and the thought of having sex before marriage made my guilty Christian penis crawl back up inside my guilty Christian body. We didn't really talk much during breakfast. I think we both realized that after all the Canada talk we didn't really have that much in common.

Me: So . . . what do you like to do?
Canadian: I like to travel around the world! You?

Me: I like to lie in bed and watch Netflix while squirting low-fat Reddi-wip into my mouth.

Ya, it wasn't a match made in heaven. But the next day was a big one. I was shooting my first short film for my YouTube channel. It was set at Christmas and was about a guy (my character) getting his first kiss. I swear I hadn't written it for personal reasons. The girl I cast was Lisa Schwartz. I had met Lisa a year before when we were working on a video together for another YouTube channel. She was sweet, pretty, and a little older than me. I say "a little older" because even though it was only by a couple of years, given my lack of sexual experience I might as well have been twelve. Although I think twelve-year-olds get more hand jobs than I did. Lisa got to the house where we were filming, and I started talking to her about the scene. I played it SUPER cool.

Me: So are you nervous to make out?!?!!!! [nervous laugh]
Lisa: Not really.
Me: Me neither!!!! [nervous laugh that ends with a small amount of pee]

It was off to a great start. So as we made our way to the front yard where we were going to kiss, I started to panic. Not only was this going to be my first kiss but it was going to be my first kiss on camera! What if I bit her? Or puked? Or swallowed her tongue? Hey, it could happen. The director yelled "action" and the time had come. She looked up at me and I looked down at her and she went in for the kiss. All I remember is thinking how much her lips felt like bologna with mayonnaise smeared on it. And that was a good thing. CUT!

Me: That wasn't so bad!
Lisa: Thanks?
Me: How did it feel?
Lisa: What?
Me: Like . . . did it feel good?
Lisa: You wear a lot of ChapStick.

SCORE! This was going great. We did a few more takes and then it was over. Afterward I went back home and my Canadian roommate was sitting on the bed waiting for me with a remote in one hand and a can of low-fat Reddi-wip in the other. She was ready to please me. As I sat on the bed I looked at her and initiated the most uncomfortable conversation imaginable.

Me: We should kiss.
Canadian: Ok!
Me: Cool. Let's do it.
Canadian: Great.

We looked at each other in silence for about thirty seconds.

Canadian: So . . . when are you going to do it?
Me: I have to do it??
Canadian: You're the guy.

Me: But today Lisa did it!

Canadian: Wait . . . how many girls have you kissed?

Me: Um . . . are we counting relatives?

Canadian: Did you have your first kiss today?

Me: Maybe.

Canadian: Wow . . . that's so sweet. And a little sad. But mostly sweet.

Me: Want to be my second?

Canadian: Sure! Thank God I'm not your first. That's too much pressure.

Me: What do you mean?

Canadian: You never forget your first kiss. You always think about what your life would have been like if you had stayed with them. It's a lot of pressure. It's like a first crush. You never get over it.

It was at that moment I started overthinking everything I had experienced that day. Was Lisa the one? Should I have whisked her off her feet and made her my wife? Should I run to her house and kiss her in the rain? Then I remembered that she was an actress who had no interest in dating a twenty-one-year-old virgin and I was sitting on a bed with a willing Canadian with a season's worth of *Hoarders* in her hand. So I went in for the kiss. And I stopped right before I hit her lips.

Canadian: What?

Me: I don't know what to do.

Canadian: Kiss me.

Me: I know that! I just mean like . . . how?

Canadian: Put your lips up against mine. Not that hard.

I reached into my pocket and applied lots of ChapStick.

Canadian: Rub that off.

Me: Huh?

Canadian: No girl wants the guy to have glossier lips than her. It's creepy.

Thanks a lot, *Seventeen* magazine! I made my way back to her lips. And stopped again.

Me: Wait. Can I start somewhere else?

Canadian: We are DEFINITELY not there yet, dude.

Me: No, not that. I want to start far away and then make my way to your lips.

So I started kissing her hand and slowly made my way up her arm. I got to her shoulder and then went up her neck. As I made my way up to her face she was trembling. This was the most romantic thing you could ever dream of, except I had NO idea it was romantic. I was just trying to calm my nerves and delay the inevitable. I finally got to her lips, and we had a pretty long kiss. As I pulled away she looked at me like I was some player who knew exactly what I was doing. In reality I knew about as much as that can of low-fat Reddi-wip in her hand. I was just lucky I guess.

We ended up dating for the next year. It wasn't the best relationship, but it was what we both needed at the time. We were both lonely and wanted someone to talk to. It was more of a friendship with some kissing thrown in. Kind of like the relationship I'd had with my grandma but more culturally acceptable. Our breakup broke the record for the most mutual parting of ways in history. Here's the text-message conversation:

Me: Hey . . . should we break up?

Canadian: Ya probably.

Me: Ok.

Canadian: Did you watch *Hoarders* last night?

Me: Ya! I can't believe that woman ate her dead dog thinking it was jerky.

Canadian: I know! Crazy!

Me: Well . . . goodbye I guess.

Canadian: Do we have to unfollow each other on Twitter? I'd rather still follow you. You have funny tweets.

Me: No way. I never unfollow anyone. That's so tacky.

Canadian: Agreed.

And that was it. I still follow her on Twitter to this day and every once in a while we fave each other's tweets. I usually only fave them if it's something about Canada. The day after we broke up I got an email from Lisa asking if I wanted to hang out. It was super random and felt like a scene in a terrible romantic comedy starring Katherine Heigl and Jon Hamm. Except Lisa's not a notorious cunt, and I have a slightly-below-average-sized penis. We ended up going to dinner and having a really great talk about relationships and life in general. She had just gotten out of a long one and I had just gotten out of an . . . immature one? We talked for hours but this time I wasn't just interested in her homeland, I was interested in her. I wanted to know all about her childhood, her family, her way of thinking about the world. It was like there was this gift in front of me and all I wanted to do was unwrap it and see what was inside. If it was as beautiful as the outside, there was no way I was going to regift it.

We stayed up till four a.m. It was one of the most magical nights I had ever had. It was even more magical than the night I watched *Titanic* three times in a row while cuddling with my mom.

Me: Well, I should probably go. You gotta get to bed.
Lisa: Ya . . . thanks for tonight. I needed this.
Me: Me too. Night.

I started to walk out the door and then I stopped myself. I wasn't going to be the pussy I had been a year ago. I was a man, and I knew what I wanted. I turned around, took her in my arms, and kissed her passionately. Sparks flew and hearts exploded. As we pulled away she looked at me and smiled.

Lisa: You aren't wearing as much ChapStick.
Me: I only put one coat on today.

Lisa: Thanks.

And to this day we are still kissing each other with the same amount of passion. It's been more than three years, and I still feel like there's more to unwrap. Every day I get a glimpse of what's inside. I hope it never ends.

THE ORIGINAL CATFISH

ABOUT THE ARTIST

Becky "Bolt" Fulford has been drawing all her life, constantly studying other artists and trying different techniques. She left school on her sixteenth birthday and is always looking for work in creative fields. She grew up in Grand Bay, Alabama, and moved to Texas at the age of eleven. Follow her on Twitter and Instagram at @bolt_tothestage.

BING. New AOL Instant Messenger message. I ran over to my old Dell laptop and pried it open. This was 2002 and Dell was the shit, so no judgment. I opened up my AIM and there it was, a picture of a flaccid ninth-grade boy's penis with the text "So baby, U like?" under it. I slammed my Dell shut and locked my bedroom door. What had I done?

Flashback to one week earlier. I had just started high school and very quickly realized that I wasn't the cool kid. I wasn't even the nerdy kid. I was the invisible kid. I can't tell you the amount of times a group of students would literally crash right through me in the hallway like they were an eighteen-wheeler truck and I was a bag of old McDonald's someone threw out the window. You would think that being morbidly obese would make me easier to see, but it somehow acted as a cloak of invisibility. My blubber must have had some kind of magical power. If there had been a sad version of the X-Men I would have been Magneto and all the special-ed kids with superior upper-body strength would have been my students.

Me being undetectable to the human eye made it particularly difficult when our teacher would divide us into groups for class assignments. Usually I wasn't even picked last; I was literally forgotten. I had a teacher ask me once if I was there to check on the air conditioner. So during the first week of school we had a project in social studies class. Our teacher wanted us to pick groups and form our own "societies." After my teacher asked if I was the janitor and I told her I was fourteen, she had me join a group of surfer kids who had a collective IQ of ten and a collective STD score of everything. I tried to make conversation with one of them.

Me: So, you watch *American Idol*?
Surfer Kid: Aren't you the cafeteria lady?

It was going great. I sank into my chair and prayed that there would be a natural disaster that would kill everyone in my school except for me. That didn't happen, so I just stared at the clock until it was time to leave. That night I went home and decided to do a little research on my group mates to see how I could get along with them. Maybe we had similar interests? Maybe they were closet homosexuals with a fat fetish? It was worth looking into. I logged on to MySpace and began my hunt. My only friends at the time were Tom and Pauly Shore, so I was pretty sure we didn't have any mutual friends. I went to each of their pages and stalked the shit out of it. During my investigation I began to realize something about these surfer kids that I had secretly suspected all along: they were horrible. Every picture they posted was of them shirtless and every comment they shared was a version of: "UR SO FUCK-ING HOT FUCK ME." Clearly we had nothing in common. The only person who had ever wanted to fuck me was a homeless lady who used to stand outside of Ralphs and tell me I had a "sad face that she wanted to sit on." I kept looking at their pages and started not only questioning how people could be so vapid but also questioning whether God exists. It was a really dark few hours.

The next day I went back to class and sat in my group once again, waiting for some kind of fatal natural disaster. I tried to strike up another conversation, and this time it lasted longer than ten seconds. Unfortunately it wasn't a friendly chat about the weather. It was a tear-inducing indictment against childhood obesity. You know, typical fourteen-year-old banter.

Me: So, what did you guys do last night?

Surfer Kid 1: Got high with my uncle and tried to get his dog drunk.

Me: Fun. What about you?

Surfer Kid 2: Fucked some chick I met on AIM.

Me: You guys have sex?

They all looked at me with dumb in their eyes and emptiness in their heads.

Me: Oh. Cool. Sometimes I think about sex. Then I get scared and pray about it.

Surfer Kid 3: I went to the gym. Almost fucked a girl there but she was a dyke or something.

Me: You go to the gym? Are you allowed at the gym? Isn't that for grown-ups and handicapped people?

Surfer Kid 3: Anybody can go to the gym.

Surfer Kid 1: Maybe you should.

The two other surfer kids let out a collective "oooooooooh."

Me: I'm fat. I get it.

Surfer Kid 1: You're like obese though. I saw an episode of *Dr. Phil* where he talked about how all the kids now are getting obese and they are going to die before graduation or some shit.

Surfer Kid 2: Damn, dog, those statistics are scary.

Me: Let's go back to not talking. That was less traumatizing.

Surfer Kid 1: Then my mom said that fat people get fat because they are lazy and hate themselves. Also that they secretly want to die so they are killing themselves slowly with food.

Surfer Kid 3: Shit. That's crazy. Fat people are sad. Is it bad that sometimes I don't even consider fat people to be people? Like, I think of them as animals or robots or something. Know what I mean?

Me: I'm right here.

Surfer Kid 1: Do you want to die?

Me: At this moment, yes. More than anything in the world.

Surfer Kid 1: I don't wanna sound like an asshole, bro, but you should stop being so fat. It's sad and you are gonna make our school look bad. 'Cause Dr. Phil said that the fattest school in America is in California and they are making them all do extra homework and stuff to make up for it.

Me: That literally makes no sense.

Surfer Kid 1: Neither does your lifestyle.

The surfer group stared at me with hate in their eyes. I broke down and started crying like a little bitch. But can you blame me? They had basically just told me to kill myself and that I was a robot or something. I told the teacher I had an emergency and had to go to the bathroom. She didn't question me. That's one plus about being a fat kid in school. Nobody questions the necessity of a trip to the bathroom. They just assume your ass is in a constant state of explosion.

I ran to the bathroom and locked myself in the stall. I cried for a good ten minutes and then took a shit. There's nothing more depressing than crying while you are smelling your own shit. It's almost as depressing as eating sandwich rolls at a funeral reception. Whoever thought a funeral reception was a good idea needs to be shot. I sat on that toilet for a good thirty minutes trying to wrap my brain around what had just happened. How could those guys be such assholes? How could I have let myself show so much weakness and not stand up to them? Why is Dr. Phil talking about other people being fat? So many questions. Next, I did what any teenager does when faced with adversity: I planned my revenge.

That night I logged back on to MySpace. How could I use their interests against them? What did they like to do? Well, from our chat that day I'd discovered that they loved drugs, animal abuse, and hooking up with girls from AIM. Then it hit me like an eighteen-wheeler through a school hallway: I could pretend to be a girl on AIM and ruin their lives.

I didn't have an AOL Instant Messenger account because the only people I talked to on a daily basis were my mom and my cat, so this technology was useless to me. So to get the plan rolling I had to sign up for AIM under a fake name and with a fake picture. I decided to go with Carol. I know. Carol kinda sounds like the name of an old drunk, but I always thought there was something sexy about it. Maybe because that homeless lady outside of Ralphs was named Carol. Anyways, my next step was to find a picture, so I went to Google Images and typed in "high school girl whore slut." Surprisingly this led to pages and pages of options. I decided to go with a simple girl with extremely large nipples. Classy and tasteful. I created her profile and started filling in all the blanks.

FAVORITE MOVIE: Fucking

FAVORITE BOOK: How to do fucking

FAVORITE SONG: Sing while you fuck me

FAVORITE ANIMAL: I fucked a dog once

FAVORITE QUOTE: "I fucked a dog once" —Carol

I was ready. The perfect girl . . . for these idiots. So I decided to start with Surfer Kid 1 since he was the guy who started the obesity debate. I went to his profile and saw his screen name was typed up in his bio, which read like an obituary for his brain.

ABOUT SURFER KID 1:

Hey, sup. I like hooka, hardcore rap, and getting head. I also like reading blogs about 9/11 conspiracies. Somethin aint right ya'll. Buildings don't just fall down like that. Hit me up on AIM: Ilikenipplerings

So I sent my first AIM message to Ilikenipplerings.

CAROLisWET: Hey.

Two minutes later, shit started going down.

Ilikenipplerings: Sup. Who dis?
CAROLisWET: Carol. I'm wet.
Ilikenipplerings: What?
CAROLisWET: I said, I'm wet.
Ilikenipplerings: Like . . . sweating?

For a guy who seemed to be all about vagina, he sure had no fucking idea how one worked.

CAROLisWET: You like boobs?
Ilikenipplerings: Ya.
CAROLisWET: Wanna see my boobs?
Ilikenipplerings: Really?
CAROLisWET: Mhmmm
Ilikenipplerings: Ya. Ok. Let me just make sure my mom's not home.

Yikes. If Carol were real that would have really dried her up.

Ilikenipplerings: K. She's not here. My little sister is but
she's in the other room watching TV.

CAROLisWET: Sounds hot.

Ilikenipplerings: Ya. I guess.

CAROLisWET: So, you wanna see my boobs?

Ilikenipplerings: Ya.

CAROLisWET: You ever had sex b4?

Ilikenipplerings: Ya. Like every day pretty much. One time
I did it in a Wendy's bathroom.

CAROLisWET: Hot. Did you eat a frostee afterwards?

Ilikenipplerings: I wanted to but I couldn't afford that AND
my bus ride.

CAROLisWET: I like a man who's responsible with money.

Ilikenipplerings: Ya. I keep it all in a jar with my name on
it. It's pretty pimp.

CAROLisWET: How about you show me something first.

Ilikenipplerings: . . . . Huh?

Ok, I know what you're thinking: this is disturbing. Trust me,
I know. But I was a fat kid scorned and I was ready to GO THERE
with no regrets. My plan was to get the most unflattering picture of this kid's dick and print out hundreds of them and post
them around school the next day. It was a genius plan. Except
for the fact that I would get expelled for doing that and possibly
go to prison for child porn, but I didn't think that far ahead.

CAROLisWET: I want to see your thing.

Ilikenipplerings: My thing?

CAROLisWET: Your penis.

Ilikenipplerings: Um . . . . why?

CAROLisWET: Cause I like penises. They are cool. And they make Carol wet.

Ilikenipplerings: Can't you just like . . . Google a picture of one?

CAROLisWET: But I want to see yours. I bet it's super. . . . . . tan?

I'm not great at sexy talk. But hey, neither was he, so we were evenly matched.

Ilikenipplerings: So like . . . if I take a pic of it and send it to you . . . you will show me your boobs?

CAROLisWET: And my vagina.

Ilikenipplerings: ?!?!?!!?!!

CAROLisWET: Yep. All 8 inches of it.

I had never seen a vagina so I assumed length was a part of it. I was incorrect.

Ilikenipplerings: K. Make me hard first.

CAROLisWET: No. I like soft penises.

Ilikenipplerings: Really? That's kinda gross.

CAROLisWET: Do you want to see me naked or not?

Ilikenipplerings: G2g. Brb.

For those of you who aren't kids of the '00s, that means "got to go" and that he'd "be right back." I took that to mean he was freaked the fuck out and was throwing his computer out the window. I felt defeated. I guess my plan wasn't perfect. Maybe I was too forceful? Maybe I wasn't as seductive as I could have been? I was just about to head to the kitchen. Then it happened.

BING.

I ran to my computer and cracked it back open. What I saw was a new picture message from Ilikenipplerings and oh dear God was it horrifying.

Ilikenipplerings: So baby, U like?

Baby didn't like, baby LOVED. It was a picture of his horrifyingly small, shriveled-up penis placed on top of his lopsided, weirdly shaped balls. If this picture was seen by anyone they would think it was a toddler with some kind of birth defect. I slammed my computer shut and locked my door. I knew this was what I'd wanted but I had the sinking feeling that I'd gone too far. I knew this kid was an asshole, but did he deserve to have his life ruined? I took the rest of the night to think about my decision. I had his adolescence in the palm of my hand and I could easily crush it if I wanted to. I decided to just print out one of the pictures and put it in my backpack. That way if he said something mean to me I could whip it out and show it to everyone and get my sweet shriveled revenge.

The next day I walked into school with my head held high. I was ready for that group of kids to knock me down in the hallway because I had something they didn't: a picture of a penis in my backpack. I went into class and sat with my surfer group.

Me: So. What did you guys do last night?

Surfer Kid 2: Got into a fight with my mom about whether or not Hamburger Helper is still Hamburger Helper if she doesn't put hamburger in it.

Me: Hmm. Intriguing.

Surfer Kid 3: I looked at my dad's porn. I found some really weird shit in his room. There was like a picture of a lady peeing into a Crock-Pot.

Me: Nice. What about you?

Surfer Kid 1: Huh?

Me: What did you do last night?

Surfer Kid 1: Oh . . . nothin'.

He looked like a train had hit him. His face was limp and pale. He looked like a guy who'd had his heart broken . . . oh shit.

Surfer Kid 2: You ok, bro?

Surfer Kid 1: Ya. I'm fine.

He wasn't fine. He was miserable. Like a puppy that had gotten its balls cut off. I didn't want to feel bad for him but unfortunately underneath all my big fat layers was an even bigger fat heart.

Surfer Kid 3: You fuck that chick from polo yet? I heard she shaves now.

Surfer Kid 1: Nah. I'm over chicks for a while.

He put his head down on his backpack and sank deeper into his depression. I felt horrible. This guy was hurting and it was my fault. I can't imagine how it must have felt to send a stranger a picture of you at your most vulnerable and have them not even respond to tell you how "not disgusting" it was. I told the teacher I had a bathroom emergency and poofed out my stomach to make it look EXTRA urgent. I ran to the bathroom and locked myself in a stall. I pulled the picture of his micro penis out of my pocket and gave it one last look. It really was disgusting. I crumpled it up and threw it in the toilet. Before I flushed I made a pact with myself that I would never stoop as low as anyone who was bullying me. The feeling I got from knowing I had hurt this asshole's heart was even worse than the feeling I got when he and his friends had called me a fat robot animal. It wasn't worth it. I flushed the toilet and went back to class feeling a little better about myself.

That night I opened up my sick Dell and deleted Carol from the internet. I didn't need her anymore. I also deleted AIM, because let's be honest, I didn't need that anymore either. I was the original catfish before catfishing was even a thing. I did it before it was a term on Urban Dictionary or a heavily scripted reality show on MTV. And from that day forward I would never again pretend to be anybody who I'm not. Instead I just Photoshop the absolute SHIT out of my own pictures to make me look like a completely different person. But hey, don't we all do that?

BETWEEN HOLLYWOOD AND AN ABORTION CLINIC

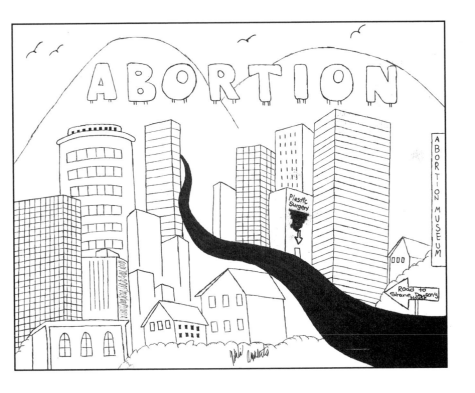

ABOUT THE ARTIST

Natalia Armenta is in the eleventh grade at California Military Institute. She has been drawing since elementary school and learned more about art in Ms. Hoxmeier's art class. She is considering a career in clothing design, or even drawing manga. She has lived most of her life in Perris, California. Follow her on Twitter at @armenta_natalia.

Every kid hopes that one day they will be walking around a mall and have a stranger in a business suit walk up to them and say, "Hey . . . You should be in the movies! I'm a big Hollywood agent. Give me a call after you finish that disgusting cheese-filled pepperoni pretzel dog." But stuff like that only happens on TV, right? Wrong. This is the story of how I was discovered in a shopping mall while stuffing my pimple-covered, eighteen-year-old face full of "frozen yogurt." I put "frozen yogurt" in quotations because let's keep it real. It's ice cream. It's sugary, topping-covered diabetes-in-a-cardboard-bucket ice cream. Watching obese people go directly from their Weight Watchers meeting to a frozen yogurt shop is like watching all those poor people fall off the sides of the *Titanic* when it was sinking. If they only knew how that cold water would kill them.

So I was walking around my local mall in Long Beach one summer afternoon in 2007. I had graduated from high school a year before that, and I was trying to figure out my next move. I had lost a shit-ton of weight and gotten my signature emo haircut, so I had my sights set on being a Disney Channel star. I even had my own catchphrase: "Hey! That's YO mama!" Trust me, in the right sitcom with the right story line it could have worked. Anyways, I was trying to find some new clothes to match my new look: young, fresh teenager. So I went into an Urban Outfitters and started searching through all the ironic T-shirts. Ten Chuck Norris references later, I decided that it might not be my store. As I was leaving, a sad-looking woman in a turtleneck and high-rise pants walked up to me and grabbed my arm.

Sad Woman: Wow. You look familiar!

Me: A lot of older women tell me I have the eyes of their ex-husbands. Well . . . that's mainly just my mom.

Sad Woman: Hey! And you're funny too!

Me: I wasn't joking, but thanks!

Sad Woman: You kind of look like that guy on TV!

Me: The "Dude, you're getting a Dell" guy? Ya, I get that a lot. Not as much anymore since he killed himself.

Sad Woman: No! I'm talking about YOU!

Me: I'm a little confused. Is this a hidden-camera show? Did you guys see me pick my ass and sniff it when I was over there looking at ironic bumper stickers? 'Cause I wasn't smelling for poop, it's just a weird habit. Probably a childhood thing. Something about loneliness and forcing unpleasantness upon my undeserving self.

Sad Woman: No, I'm trying to tell you that you should BE on TV! Are you an actor?

Me: Ya! I was in my high school musical!

Sad Woman: Great! What part?

Me: Fat guy with no song.

Sad Woman: Wow! That's . . . specific.

Me: Ya, I really made it my own.

Sad Woman: Well I'm from a big-time acting academy where we have young actors come audition for us and if we like them we get them big Hollywood agents!

Me: Wow, you're like a junk email come to life!

Sad Woman: Seriously! It's legit! I have a card and everything!

She pulled out a business card for a company called Juan Casablancas. It was laminated and everything. It even had some nice clip art next to her name. This wasn't some homemade shit. This was AT LEAST made at Kinko's. I instantly trusted her.

Sad Woman: Come to the audition tomorrow. I'll tell everyone you're coming. And bring that star quality!

As she walked away I had an inkling of "Oh shit, she's going to rape and murder me," but I also had an inkling that "Hey! That's YO mama!" could finally become a reality. So I took my chances and walked into the nearest teenybopper store and found the most Disney Channel outfit I could find!

The next day I pulled up to a shady building somewhere in Orange County. It was two hours from Hollywood and also housed a divorce paralegal office and a Planned Parenthood, so I should have known that this wasn't going to be my ticket to fame. I got out of my car and checked my reflection in the window.

Emo hair swoop greased down to my forehead: *check*
Unflattering vest with decorative shredded trim: *check*
Jeans so skinny you could see the outline of my unimpressive, flaccid grower: *check*
Endless amounts of sadness and desperation in my eyes: *double check*

As I entered the elevator that smelled like abortion, I looked around at my fellow desperate wannabe stars, mostly terrified-looking kids with their parents. One girl told her dad she felt like she was going to throw up and her dad told her to swallow it. As I watched a twelve-year-old girl vomit in her mouth and then swallow it, I started to second-guess whether or not I should be there. The elevator finally opened and in front of me I saw a big lobby covered in movie posters and pictures of famous people. There was a flat-screen showing Beyoncé's world tour and there were dishes filled with candy everywhere. None of that hard butterscotch shit. We're talking Reese's and mini Twix. I didn't even know they MADE mini Twix. All my apprehensions were gone, and I was ready for this Hollywood life.

We were all escorted to the sitting area, which looked like a mini movie theater. There was a stage and a big screen playing clips of *That's So Raven* and *Lizzie McGuire*. I started mingling with the others and realized that something was fishy.

Me: So, how did you guys get invited to this?
Vomit Girl: A lady told me I should be on TV. She also said
    I was prettier than Hannah Montana.

Note: the girl had a lazy eye and some kind of skin disease
that made her look slightly reptilian.

Me: Really? Wow. That's . . . nice.
Vomit Girl: Ya. I don't want to be an actor but my dad said
    I need to do it because he has a lot of legal bills.
Vomit Girl's Dad: Car accident. Killed a guy. His fault. You
    know how it goes.
Me: Totally.

Obviously this wasn't a room full of talented undiscovered
stars. It was a room full of sad, desperate people who were bor-
derline suicidal. I saw a mom eating her own hair. She actually
ripped out a strand from her head, rolled it around her fingers till
it formed a ball, and ate it. A loud feedback sound rang through
the speakers and scared the shit out of everyone. It was the sad-
looking turtleneck woman I had met at the mall. She was holding
on to the microphone doing her best Ryan Seacrest impression.

Sad Woman: Ladies and gentlemen, who's ready to find
    the next superstar!

Everyone cheered. Except Vomit Girl. She had vomit in her
mouth.

Sad Woman: Great! Well, let's get started! Here's how it's going to go. Everyone here is going to come up onstage one by one and read a short commercial off that cue card! After me and the judges see all your auditions we will decide who is ready for part two of the competition!

So it started. One by one we would go up onstage and perform the worst-written commercial ever and then sit back in our seats and wait for our fate to be determined. I was up last. I got up onstage and read that cue card like a champion.

Me: I don't know about you but I love food. It's my favorite thing! But who has the time to make it? Not me! That's why I bought the Food Maker. It makes food! Buy one today!

I even took an invisible bite of a sandwich and moaned a little.

Vomit Girl's Dad: Damn, he's good.

After I got offstage the turtleneck woman went up to the mic and started calling people's names. She called about ten out of the thirty people who were there. My name was one of the lucky ten. The other twenty people left in tears, and I sat awaiting part two of this challenge.

Sad Woman: Shane, let's start with you. Come back to the office with me. I want you to meet someone.

I fixed my hair, checked my breath, picked my ass and smelled it, and was on my way. As I walked into one of the many offices down the hallway I met a small man named Allan. He was flamboyant and loudly dressed. He even had a mug in his left hand that said: "I'm bringing SASSY back." I instantly trusted him.

Allan: So, you are the Sean I've been hearing so much about.

Me: Actually my name is Shane.

Allan: I know. I was testing you to see if you would correct me. And you did. You failed.

Me: Oh. Sorry.

Allan: Don't be sorry. Be a welcome mat. Let people walk all over you. Feel the pain of Hollywood and then once you've had enough you can start to walk all over them! Make them bleed and feel sorry for EVERYTHING THEY EVER DID TO YOU.

Me: Are we still talking about me?

Allan: Sorry, sometimes my passion gets the better of me. I've also had about eight cups of coffee and three muscle relaxers, so I'm all jazzed up. Let's get back to YOU.

Me: Well, I want to be an actor.

Allan: Get out of my office.

Me: Huh?

Allan: Get the fuck out! NOW! How dare you come into

MY place of work and tell me that you WANT something!

Me: Is this the muscle relaxers talking or . . .

Allan: Don't tell me you WANT to be an actor. Tell me you ARE an actor. Don't WANT! BE!

Me: Ooooooh. Wow, you really should get that printed on a mug.

Allan: I already did. I sell them on Etsy. Signed.

Me: So, you think I could make it?

Allan: Baby, with me on your side, I can make you the next Mitchel Musso.

Note: Mitchel Musso was a thing in 2007. I know most of you have no idea who that is but trust me, he was a thing.

Allan: All you have to do is sign up for this set of classes and when we think you're ready we will set up a meeting for you with a big Hollywood agent.

Me: Great! Sign me up!

Allan: That's the spirit! It will be three thousand dollars, and please make it out to "cash."

Me: WHAT?!

Allan: Hey, it pays to be famous. And trust me, kid, you got FAME in your future. If you were a mug, you would have FAME written all over you.

I know what you're thinking: "It's a scam." Why would anyone pay $3,000 to take classes from a dude who sells mugs on Etsy? Because desperation makes people do crazy things.

I went home and told my mom about the entire experience and even though deep down in her heart she probably knew it was a scam, she wanted me to fulfill my dream so badly that it didn't matter. We were pretty poor at the time so she had to max out every credit card she could find. I think we even had to get my grandmother to chip in. All I could think about was getting rich and famous and getting my family out of the hellhole we were living in. My parents divorced when I was nine and they both filed for bankruptcy, so since then it had been a daily struggle to make ends meet. That vomit girl and I weren't so different after all. We just wanted out of our current situation. I wanted to be on TV and be a star, and she wanted her dad not to go to prison for manslaughter.

The next week I went in for my first class. I looked around at my fellow students and I noticed a lot of them were from the group of twenty who were told to leave after the audition. I asked one of them why they were there and they said, "Oh, they called me later and said that I was actually in the top ten but they didn't want to tell me till later to toughen up my skin." That's the moment I knew all of this bullshit was a fraud. The posters on the walls, the Beyoncé tour playing on a flat-screen, the good candy. It was all a cover-up for some scam where con artists sucker desperate parents into paying thousands of dollars for bullshit classes. And I fell for it. Hard.

A tall, model-looking woman walked out in front of the class and introduced herself as the teacher for the day. Her name was Neve and she looked like she'd stepped out of a magazine. I was yet again sucked back into the scam and eating up every word.

Neve: Hello, class. I'm going to teach you how to walk like a model today. Who here knows how to walk?

All the students laughed. Although this would have been SUPER awkward if anyone was in a wheelchair.

Neve: Good. Stand up and let's see what you got.

So the rest of the students (who were all under the age of twelve) and I started walking back and forth across the room while Neve judged us like horses. She was yelling things like "Straighten your back! Stop smiling! Suck in that ass!" I'm not sure how one can "suck in that ass," but you better believe I tried my hardest. After we did our walk she lined us up and started critiquing our "looks." She got to me and let me have it. She told me that my teeth were too yellow. My arms were too white. And the thing that really stung?

Neve: That hair. What is with that hair? You need to cut it all off or you will NEVER get anywhere in Hollywood.

From that point on I knew this woman was no longer to be trusted. Even I, with all my self-hatred, knew that my emo hair was in style and very marketable to a young audience.

This chick was a fraud. And it took her making fun of my hair to show me that. After class I walked back to Allan's office to have a one-on-one with him. A few teachers tried to stop me but I was like a pregnant lady making my way through Disneyland looking for a turkey leg. People were going to either get the fuck out of my way or be killed. I opened his door and let myself in.

Me: I need to talk to you.

Allan: You seem angry. Here, have a mini Twix.

Me: NO! There's no amount of miniature candies or clever mugs that could change my mood right now! You guys are a FRAUD!

Allan: GASP! Who is this? Because the Juan I know would never say such accusatory things!

Me: My name is SHANE and I want my mom's money back!

Allan: Ok, I see that you are upset. Use it. Let's do a mono-logue. Have you ever seen the Tom Hanks movie where he finds out he has AIDS? There's a scene in there I think you could NAIL right now. Let me print it out!

Me: NO! No monologues! No Mitchel Musso comparisons! I want my money back NOW!

Allan: Cynthia, can you shut the door?

A tiny hand shut the door and Allan motioned for me to have a seat.

Allan: Yes. We are a business. We need people who are will-ing to pay big bucks to get a ticket to Hollywood. And yes, some of the other children are hopeless and their parents probably should have visited the business next door years ago if you know what I'm sayin'. But there are some of you who are talented who we really are going to help out. You are one of the lucky few. We are going to get you the best agent we can find and I promise you, a year from now you are going to be winning a Teen Choice Award and we will be in the audience cheering you on.

Me: So you're telling me that you KNOW some of the kids out there are hopeless?

Allan: I'm telling you some of those kids out there smell like abuse and it turns me on.

He let out a small laugh. I didn't. I got up.

Me: You are a horrible, horrible person and I hope you get all the bad karma that you deserve.

Allan: Wow. Looks like you're the one who's bringing SASSY back!

Me: I hope you enjoy your life.

Allan: Wait. Ok, I'll give you your money back. I'll even set you up with one of my agent friends. Deal?

I took the deal. But I also walked out of the room and told all the other students' parents what a scam the company was. Unfortunately none of them cared. The slight glimmer of hope that all those movie posters on the walls were giving them was enough to blind them to reality. A year later I decided to go to their website to see if Allan still worked there and what I found wasn't shocking at all. The company had gone under because of all the legal fees they weren't able to keep up with due to all the lawsuits from their former students. I breathed a sigh of relief. Karma does always come back around. And a few years after that when I won a Teen Choice Award for Choice Web Star I thought about all the people who had helped me get there. And not one of those people was Allan or anyone from that shitty acting academy next to the abortion clinic.

DENNY'S AND DEATH

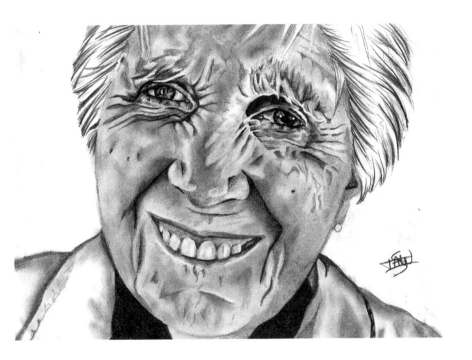

ABOUT THE ARTIST

Ivy Sangers is eighteen years old and studying journalism in Utrecht, a province in the Netherlands. She has been drawing ever since she was a little girl, and her main interest is painting portraits. Follow her on Twitter at @Ivys_.

The smell of Denny's at three a.m. reminds me of two things: (1) burning-hot diarrhea rushing out of my swollen hole and (2) the death of my grandmother. The first one is pretty obvious. I mean, they have an entire menu dedicated to "BACON-IZING" and "CHEESIFYING" their food. That just sounds like anal leakage. The second is because that's where I was the night I waited for my grandmother to die. I know, it sounds morbid, but it's the truth.

It was a night of me and my brother Jerid constantly checking our phones to see if we had a text from our mom saying "She's gone" and then some kind of terribly conceived sad-face emoticon. Most likely something like "8*{" or even something like "#(P&." I've gotten that emoticon from her before. I have no idea what it stands for but it can't be good.

I was twenty-one years old, and I had just moved out of my mom's house and gotten an apartment with my older brother, so our phones were usually filled with texts from her every morning. Usually about a dream she'd had in which we'd both died a violent death, and she was just checking to see if we were ok. You guessed it, I got my calm, rational personality from my mother.

My grandmother was a pretty healthy woman considering

she lived on a diet of fat-free cookies and old-people candy, so when she was admitted to the hospital it was a shock to us all. She complained of her legs hurting, so we figured she had torn a muscle from too much running to the toilet (my bowel issues are genetic). But the doctor said she needed to stay overnight for additional testing. She took it as a mini vacation and wasn't worried at all, and neither were we. Old people go to the hospital all the time! Unfortunately it was more serious than we thought. The next morning I had a voice mail on my phone from my mom. She was calling from the hospital, and I could tell it was serious because it didn't start with her singing some kind of Weird Al parody song.

"Shane. Call me when you get this. Grandma's not doing well. I think this is it."

I'll never forget that voice mail. It hit me in the gut like a BACONIZED CHEESIFIED quadruple burger. I was numb. I ran into my brother's room without even knocking on the door to make sure he had time to cover his morning erection. He jumped out of bed when I told him the news and we rushed out of the apartment like it was on fire.

My brother and I had a very special bond with my grandma. Most of the happy memories I have from childhood involve her. She had a shitty attitude and hated everything. She watched trashy TV shows and yelled at the screen. She was a night eater and left the bathroom door open while she did her butt business. She was my soul mate. One of my favorite memories was when my brother and I dressed her up as 50 Cent and had her repeat his incredibly racist and demeaning lyrics on camera. I always thought I'd want to show that video at her funeral but she had a black friend, so when the day finally came I decided it would have been all kinds of awkward.

But back to that awful morning. My brother and I hopped in the car and sped down the freeway like we were in a shitty Nicolas Cage action movie. We almost killed about eight people, but it would have been worth it. If I didn't say good-bye to Grandma before she passed I knew I would never be able to forgive myself. I had so many things I wanted to say to her. I had so many selfies I wanted to take with her. (She loved a good selfie. #NOFILTER of course.)

We got to the hospital and ran up to her room faster than we had ever run before. It was like there was a drug dog chasing us and our asses were packed with coke. I was completely unprepared for what I saw when we finally got to her room. She wasn't watching trashy TV and yelling at the screen. She wasn't treating the nurses like waitresses at TGI Fridays. She wasn't doing her butt business with the bathroom door open. She was lying on a stiff cold bed with a tube down her throat and a machine pumping oxygen into her lungs. She was a shell of the woman I knew. I had no idea who this woman was. The woman I had seen just the night before was fun, loud, slightly prejudiced. But she was gone.

I broke down into tears and had to leave the room. I did the only thing I knew to do: vlog. I went into the bathroom and took out my iPhone and started talking to it. I talked about how scared I was to lose her. How mad I was at God for doing this. How horrible hospital bathrooms smelled. I spilled my guts and it made me feel slightly better.

About an hour later I went back into the room and the rest of my family was standing by her bedside. We aren't the chattiest of families so the awkward silence wasn't all that awkward. Nobody knew what to say. What can you say? The doctor walked in and gave us the lowdown.

"She has a lack of salt that caused her body to shut down. She has a few days left. I'm so sorry. If you're hungry there are TERRIBLE snacks in the cafeteria that are covered in arm hair from the 'cook.'"

Ok, that last half might not be exactly what he said, but you get the gist. So we waited by her bedside for the next few days. We tried to entertain ourselves by playing I Spy, but the game gets kinda depressing when all you have to "spy" are urine tubes, poop bags, and a half-dead person. So we mainly just played on our phones. After a few nights my brother and I decided to eat our emotions and Denny's sounded like just the place to do it. At three a.m. there were plenty of hookers, hobos, and drunken teenagers to keep us company. We ordered pretty much everything on the menu, including something called a "Spice to MEAT Ya." After eating that disaster I thought I would for sure die before my grandma.

BEEP BEEP.

A text. My brother and I made eye contact. Who's gonna look at their phone first? Who wants to get the sad news and tell the other one? Maybe we should just get another "Spice to MEAT Ya" and go into a food coma.

RING RING.

A text and now a PHONE CALL? Nobody calls anyone anymore unless someone is LITERALLY DEAD. This couldn't be good. I answered my phone and it was my mom. "Grandma's awake! She's sitting up in her bed eating meat loaf and complaining that the nurses all look like ninety-nine-cent-store cashiers! She's back!"

Two miracles happened that night. The first being my grandma's resurrection and the second that my ass didn't bleed from all the beige food I shoved down my face hole. We rushed back to the hospital and there she was, the woman I hadn't seen in three days, sitting upright and asking for someone to turn on "that show about that midget family." I cried happy tears as I flipped through the channels to find TLC. That night we had so much fun. We laughed, cried, and showed my grandma countless viral videos of people falling down and getting hurt. It was truly one of the best nights I had ever had with her. And then I was hit with reality.

"Can I talk to you for a minute?" the doctor said with a look on his face like he had just accidentally aborted my first child.

I walked out into the waiting room with him—my brother and mom were in the bathroom—and he told me something that took every ounce of happiness out of my body and replaced it with the feeling of jagged pieces of broken glass.

Doctor: Your grandmother hasn't taken a turn for the better I'm afraid.
Me: But she's up! And miserable! She's her old self again!

Doctor: Shane, sometimes when a person is dying there is a period of time when they become conscious so they can give their families closure. It's a phenomenon, and we really can't explain it.

Me: Wait . . . so is she already dead? Is that a ghost? A demon? AN ALIEN?! I'm so fucking confused and the CHEESIFIED milkshake I had is starting to make me hallucinate.

Doctor: No, that's your grandmother. She doesn't know she's dying. She doesn't feel pain. Her brain is blocking all of that. She is enjoying her last night with her family and when she falls asleep, she'll pass.

GREAT. Now I had to tell my mom and brother that grandma actually wasn't well, she was just having a supernatural experience like she was a character in some kind of terrible Kirk Cameron Christian movie. Thanks, doctor! You really know how to bring down the mood. Good thing you aren't in the children's ward, you DREAM CRUSHER.

So when my mother and brother came back I told them what was going on. They weren't surprised. My mom had seen somebody die before and my brother had watched A LOT of documentaries about death, so they'd both had a feeling that was what was happening. So one by one we went into the room and had a conversation with Grandma and tried to get as much closure as we could.

I thanked her for everything she had done for me. She was the reason I started acting. She was the reason I had a sliver of confidence in myself. She was the reason I smiled as a kid. When I was scared of my mom and dad's fighting I would run up to her room upstairs and she would hold me for hours. There wasn't a bruise she didn't kiss or a cut she didn't spray with HORRIBLY PAINFUL MEDICINE. She meant everything to me and then some.

My brother and mother had some time with her and then around midnight she fell asleep. We all stood and watched her. The waiting game was happening again. A few hours later her heart was still beating. She wasn't letting go. I asked the doctor how long he thought she had and he said it was up to her. If she was holding on to something it could take a while. I knew what I had to do.

I asked my brother and mother for a moment alone with her. I sat by her side and I held her hand. I whispered to her.

Me: Grandma? Are you there?

She replied in soft, almost inaudible whispers.

Grandma: Shaney?
Me: Do you know that you are dying?
Grandma: Yes.
Me: Are you scared?
Grandma: Yes.
Me: Is it because you don't want to go to hell?

Silence. Then a tear fell from her closed eye. My grandma

wasn't always the most pleasant woman to be around through-out her life, and I'm sure she was feeling a lot of guilt about that.

> Me: You might have been kind of a bitch to a lot of people in your life, but to me you were my rock. You protected me. You made me feel special and never judged me. God is so proud of you and you have nothing to be afraid of.

She gave me a small smile. Her eyes were still closed. There wasn't much life left in her but there was enough to hear me.

> Me: Is there anything else you're afraid of?

She squeezed my hand as hard as she could, which was still gentler than a toddler.

> Me: Are you scared to leave me and Jerid?
> Grandma: You need me.

I burst into tears. She was right. I needed her so badly. I was just beginning to become successful on YouTube, and I was nervous about what my life was going to turn into. My brother was just getting his life together and needed her pep talks. But we needed to let her go.

> Me: Grandma, I love you so much. But I want you to let go and not worry about us. We'll be fine. And you can

watch over us every day and make sure that we are on the right track.

Another tear from her beautiful, peacefully closed eye.

Me: It's going to be so much better up there. You're gonna fly and shit! That's insane! I've always wanted to fly. You can come hang out with me in my dreams and do all that cool angel stuff that we learned about from that terrible *Touched by an Angel* show that we used to watch together.

She smiled. God, that show was terrible.

Grandma: Thank you, Shaney. I love you.
Me: I love you so much.

I kissed her hand and she ran her fingers through my hair. After a few peaceful minutes I went into the waiting room and told my brother to go in and talk to her. They had a private conversation. I'm sure it was similar to ours and just as special. We felt at peace with the situation so we went home to get some sleep. My mother wanted to stay the night and be by her side. The next morning we got a phone call from my mom saying that she'd passed that morning. She even opened her eyes and said, "I'll always be there for you guys," before she left. I feel bad that I wasn't there for her last breath but I also feel like the moment we had shared the night before was so special that nothing could top that. And to this day I will never forget the feeling of her hand squeezing mine. And every time I go into a Denny's at three a.m., which is frequently, I know she's there sitting in the booth next to me dreading the diarrhea that's bound to come.

I love you, Grandma. Always.

MY BIRTHDAY SUIT

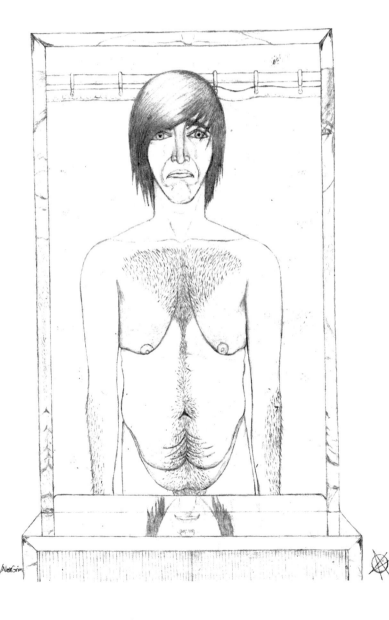

ABOUT THE ARTIST

Alex Grim *is a multitalented artist from Portland, Oregon. He grew up all around the United States. In Pensacola, Florida, at the age of five, he knew he wanted to draw seriously, with encouragement from his mother, after failing to draw a cat with a crayon in kindergarten. Primarily a sculptor now at age forty-two, Alex picked up the drawing pencil again after a nine-year hiatus . . . just for Shane. Follow him on Twitter at @AlexGrim.*

I'm going to start this off by saying I am not a fan of swimwear. Any way you look at it, it's underwear that you pee into. The material always feels like rejected scraps from a shitty Halloween costume and whoever thought using Velcro instead of zippers was a good idea needs to be shot. Up until I was eighteen I had never even tried on a swimsuit. My outfit of choice at the local pool was jean shorts and a shirt I could really get lost in. Sometimes when I lie in bed I can still hear the suction sound of my fingers pulling my wet shirt from the deep cleavage between my boy tits. One time I even wore my grandmother's muumuu to the beach. I'm not gonna lie, getting out of the water with all that wet polyester clinging to my curves made me feel like Bo Derek in *10*. If my grandmother and I had sported that muumuu side by side in a trashy magazine I think I would have gotten the coveted "Wore It Best" title, but I digress.

On my eighteenth birthday I stood naked in front of my zit-cream-covered mirror and stared at my body. Really STARED. I was a man now, and I wanted to see what I was working with. Sure, I had great hair (thank you, Mom) and extremely hairy shoulders (fuck you, Dad), but what I couldn't stop staring at was my loose skin. After high school I lost around 150 pounds, and I still had all the stretched-out, saggy skin. My body looked like that painting with all those melting clocks. My droopy chest and hangy stomach were like cartoon frowny faces. Of course when I would lie down I looked like a fucking supermodel. I'd just tuck all that skin under my back and armpits and suddenly transform into a Greek god. But as I stood in that mirror and saw that frowny face staring back at me I realized I had to do something about it.

My first idea was to use duct tape. Now, for some reason my family had duct tape at our disposal at all times in my house. I'm not sure why. Were we getting ready to kidnap a girl who was visiting shore during her family cruise? Were we trying to tape up all the wicker furniture I had broken over the years? Whatever the reason, we had a SHIT-TON of it. So I grabbed three rolls, locked my bedroom door, and started shaping. I was like an artist working on a sculpture. Working all my clay into a form that could pass as a normal human body when clothed. Each long piece of tape was wrapped tighter than the last. I got to the end of the third roll and looked in the mirror, and what I saw wasn't the Greek god I was hoping for. I looked more like a can of pastry dough that had popped open in a few places.

The tape was a failure, but luckily I got rid of all that shoulder hair when I had to RIP OFF THREE ROLLS' WORTH OF INDUSTRIAL-GRADE DUCT TAPE FROM MY FUCKING SKIN. After that I made a few more failed attempts at creating my dream body. Some involved Saran wrap, chip clips, a child's wet suit from Target, even superglue. That last one didn't end too well. But then an idea so genius, so inventive, so . . . emotionally scarring popped into my head. My mother's one-piece swimsuit.

I have so many memories of my mother's swimsuit. Even as a young kid I remember wondering, "Is my mom a whore?" The suit was tight, black, and had an open back. It even had a little keyhole in the front to show off that belly button but still hide the C-section scar. It was tasteful yet sensual. One time I even found a suggestive picture of her wearing it in a box labeled DIVORCE STUFF in the hallway closet. She hadn't worn it for years so I figured the baton should be passed. It was time to give that suit a new story. A new master. It was time to give that suit its second life. So I waited till she was at work and snuck into her room and started hunting. I looked in every drawer of every dresser, and I couldn't find it. Although I did find some of her eighties spandex workout clothes, which were a SOLID plan B. I went to the hallway closet and looked in a box marked GOODWILL and there it was. The tight black suit with the worn-out crotch pad. Side note: What is that crotch pad for? Is it to protect the vagina from the impact of a big wave? Or maybe to have a stronger barrier between vagina and sand? I can imagine how uncomfortable a sandy vagina is. Almost as uncomfortable as when sand would get in my loose under-boob skin. See, women, I relate to you.

I grabbed the suit and ran to my room. This time I left the door unlocked. I was kind of an exhibitionist. I slipped one leg in, then the other, and hoisted it up all the way to my hairless shoulders. I packed in all the skin like I was tucking a king-sized bedsheet into a twin-sized mattress. I stood up straight and looked in the mirror, and the results were more beautiful than I had ever imagined. If you squinted one eye and kind of went lazy with the other, I looked like a normal guy wearing a black tank top.

I put on my jeans and threw on a T-shirt and looked in the mirror once again. This was the first time in years that I had worn just a T-shirt. Usually it was a big sweatshirt, to hide my body, or a cargo jacket with lots of pockets. But that day, my eighteenth birthday, it was just a shirt. I heard a honk and ran outside to show off my new body. It was my friends, ready to take me out for my big celebration: Denny's and Knott's Berry Farm. Hey, I grew up in Long Beach, what did you expect?

"Shane, nice shirt!" I still remember my friend complimenting me when I got in the backseat. I casually replied, "Oh, thanks. I dunno. Got it from Target or whatever." The truth was I had gotten it at Macy's months before and had been saving it for when my body was flat enough to wear it. And it cost about $30 by the way. Ya, it was an investment in my future. So we drove to the amusement park and the whole time talked about what rides we were gonna go on. I hadn't been on that many of them because I was always too afraid I wasn't going to fit. I had been kicked off a roller coaster back when I was fat, so the thought of getting on one again was horrifying. Almost as horrifying as having to wear my mother's pre-divorce one-piece under my clothes.

When we got out of the car I felt the wind flowing through my shirt, and I made an audible "ahhhh" sound. It was probably creepy to my friends, but to me feeling the air that close to my body was a sensation I had only dreamed of. We walked to the front gates and got out our tickets. We had printed them at home because that was the cool thing to do. That and sneaking your own candy into the park. I think I had about three packs of peanut butter cups tucked in my crotch pad. Thanks, Mom.

"NEXT!" the security guard shouted as we made our way up to the front of the line. I noticed that people were having to take off their jackets and hats because they were setting the metal detectors off. "Thank God I'm not wearing a jacket like I used to!" I thought to myself. "Thank God all I have on is my . . . oh wait . . . oh God." I ran my fingers down my back and noticed my mother's swimsuit had a METAL CLASP. What did that mean? Was I going to have to take off my shirt? How would I explain to a security guard that I wasn't packing a knife, I was just wearing my mother's swimsuit underneath my clothes?! Not only were all my friends with me but literally everyone from my old high school worked there! At that moment I started planning my escape. Should I fake a heart attack? CRAP, that only worked when I was fat. Ok, what about pretending to have a seizure? That's a thing, right? Spontaneous seizures?

As I was about to make my choice I heard the dreaded "NEXT!" and had to face my fears head-on. First the security guard patted me down. I'm gonna be honest, I was excited. I'm sure to him he was just patting down a normal dude, but to me I was a NORMAL DUDE! He was probably not feeling any of my extra skin. He probably thought I just had a normal body.

Maybe even pecs? Granted, it was just my boob skin protruding outward, but hey, if he thought it was pecs I wasn't gonna fight him. Then came the metal detector. Thank God the suit was water resistant, because the sweat was pouring.

BEEP. "Are you hiding anything, man?" His eyebrows furrowed at me like I was packing something dangerous.

"Only three packs of peanut butter cups, but you can't blame me, the prices on snacks here are pretty ridiculous!" I laughed uncontrollably for a good twenty seconds.

"Turn around, kid."

I turned around, facing my friends, who were all laughing. One said, "UH-OH! He's gonna FRISK YOU! Happy eighteenth birthday!" I know I should have been scared of getting a gloved finger up my ass but I was more afraid of him seeing that I had on Kirstie Alley's Oprah Reveal outfit underneath my clothes.

"I'm just gonna lift up your shirt a little. Is that ok?"

NO! IT'S NOT OK! If you lift up my shirt then everyone here is going to see my keyhole cutout and there's no way I can pretend like it's just an undershirt I got at Target! Who would believe that Target sells undershirts with keyhole cutouts?!

But of course I said, "Ok. Sure. Just not too high. I have backne." Nice save.

His hands lifted my shirt up in the back and he paused. Confused. "What is this?" he asked under his breath.

"It's a swimsuit. Aren't there water rides here?" Another nice save.

"Ya but . . . Isn't this like . . . for chicks?"

My heart started racing. My friends were trying to read our lips.

"What's going on?! Hurry up, Shane!" one of my friends screamed as I literally diarrhead myself in panic.

"I'm going to go get my boss and make sure this is ok. Hold on."

YOUR BOSS?! Why do we need to bring more people into this? Why can't this be a quick and easy embarrassing moment? Why do we have to make it a whole fucking spectacle?! This is getting ridiculous. I wish I had stuck with the tape.

"Excuse me, sir, can you please lift up your shirt?" said the boss, who was filing her nails while she was investigating the situation.

Obviously it's not that serious so WHY ARE WE DOING IT?

"Sure, ma'am." I lifted up the back of my shirt slightly.

"More please." So I did. "More." I pulled up again. "Sir, I need to see the whole back."

WHY?! Do you really think I have a knife taped to my spine?! 'Cause if I did I would have already KILLED MYSELF WITH IT.

"Sure." I slowly lifted, trying to keep the keyhole cutout in the front covered up. But I was moving too slowly and the boss had a lot of NOTHING to get back to, so she grabbed my shirt and ripped it up.

Gasp. Shock. Confused noises. All of these things coming out of my friends' mouths. Then came the boss's laughter. "OH MY GOD! YOU WEARING A WOMAN'S SWIMSUIT?! YOU A

KINKY MOTHAFUCKA, AIN'T YOU?!" The boss thought this was the funniest thing she'd ever seen. I didn't know what would be more embarrassing, telling the truth or just going along with the kinky story.

"He's free to go. Have fun in there, beautiful!"

Well I'm glad SHE had a blast, because now it was time for me to explain to my friends what had just happened. I stood to the side while they got checked for metal materials and of course all of them were clean. As they walked up to me my heart started racing. I thought I was going to pass out. Blood started rushing to my head, and I was sweating. What was I going to say when they asked me why I was wearing a woman's swimsuit?

"Who's ready to ride the Boomerang?!" one of my friends screamed. A collective yell of excitement came from the rest of the group as they headed toward the first ride. They didn't ask. They didn't care. They were my friends, and it didn't matter to them. A tear fell from my eye as I screamed, "LET'S DO IT!" We ran into the park and had an awesome day.

Thanks, Mom, for my birthday suit.

INTERNET FAMOUS

ABOUT THE ARTIST

Sophie Lubos is currently in her freshman year at Tupelo High School. She has loved art ever since she was little. She is now taking private art classes with Daphne Works. Follow her on Twitter at @im_a_chobits.

It was nine o'clock on a Saturday night, and I was dining at an incredibly fancy restaurant eating incredibly fancy food with my incredibly sophisticated friends. Ok, I'm lying. We were eating shitty cheap Mexican food with what was probably dog meat in the taco filling and talking about all the times we had "carted." For those of you who don't know, "carted" is a term used to describe the classy act of simultaneously cumming and farting. It was a very in-depth conversation that went on for about two hours and two baskets of chips too long. As I was midstory about one incident during which my dog licked my butthole while I was masturbating and I didn't push him away (come on, we've all been there), a table nearby started yelling my name. I turned to look and what I saw was a familiar sight. It was a few teenagers with their incredibly confused parents.

Teenagers: SHANE!!!
Parents: Who's that?
Teenagers: The guy from the internet!

That conversation between child and parent doesn't go too well when the child isn't actually a teen. I've had way too many eight-year-olds scream, "That's the man from the internet!" to their parents in the middle of a crowded Target. Luckily, this time it was sweet and innocent and appropriate, so I walked over to the table and took pictures with them. Little did I know this wouldn't be the last table of people who would notice me that night. The next group wouldn't be so nice. But I'll get to that later.

The whole idea of being recognized in public is something that I never imagined would ever happen to me, much less that I'd be comfortable with it. As a kid all I wanted was to be invisible. Not because I wanted to sneak into my guy friends' rooms to compare their dick sizes to mine but because I didn't want anyone to notice me. I was never the class clown, and I did everything I could to make myself blend into the background. Whenever I went to a store I would try to color-coordinate my outfit to the store's color scheme so I could blend into the walls. That didn't always work out well, because customers would assume I was an employee and constantly ask me for help, which was the opposite of being invisible and also the opposite of fun. I can't tell you how many old women I had to help reach the "elderly pads" on the back shelf at Target. I threw ALL my red shirts away after that.

The first time I was recognized for my YouTube videos was when I was eighteen years old, and I was going to the doctor to get a physical. This was the first time I had let a doctor see my goodies so I was extremely nervous going into it. I'd spent an hour that morning manscaping in my bathroom. I wasn't very good at it. My razor was so covered in blood, you would have thought it had telekinetic powers.

At the doctor's office I sat in the waiting room and stared at my blank phone pretending to read a text. This was before there were apps, so it was a lot harder to pretend you were busy. I can't imagine standing in an elevator now next to a stranger and not having apps to help me avoid eye contact! Sounds horrible!

The doctor's assistant walked out to greet me, and she had an expression on her face I had never seen before. It was the look of someone who had just seen a dead person or a leprechaun. She appeared to be in shock and didn't move for a good five seconds. Man, I wish I'd had an app. Those five seconds felt like an eternity.

Assistant: Oh my God. You're Shane Dawson.
Me: Hi. Do I know you?

At the time my videos weren't getting very many views. I probably only had around five thousand subscribers and the only people who left comments were family members and people telling me to "get AIDS and die" . . . so it was basically just family and friends.

Assistant: Ya! I watch your videos!!
Me: You do?!
Assistant: Yup! Every week! My screen name is RachelPflower!
Me: Oh! I think I've seen you in the comments! Are you the one who told me to sit on a sword and kill myself?
Assistant: No.
Me: Oh . . . I hope I get to meet that person one day. I'm sure he's lovely.

Assistant: So what are you doing here??

Me: Getting a physical.

Then reality hit me. As I told her I was getting a physical her face went from "I just saw a leprechaun" to "I'm a cartoon dog and I just saw a cartoon steak." Her eyes were wide and her mouth was practically foaming. Was this fan going to get to see my . . . everything?? This was too much. This was much more than taking a selfie, this was showing her an everything-ie! I tried to keep cool, hoping that maybe it was just her job to send me on to the examination room and then to leave me alone with the doctor to do our uncomfortable business.

Assistant: Well, come on back!

I followed her to the doctor's office and she asked me to sit on the bench. She took a gown out of the closet and handed it to me.

Assistant: Here, change into this. And leave the back undone so the doctor can have easy access to your anus.

She left the room and I froze. I don't even think I had an anus at this point. I was so full of nerves that it had completely closed up. I tried to compose myself and put on my horribly unflattering gown. Just as I finished changing, the assistant walked back in.

Assistant: Ok, the doctor will be in soon. I'm just going to check your vitals really quickly.

She sat on a stool and swiveled over to me. She got so close that her knee was up against my poorly shaven balls. The only thing between her knee and my sad sack was a gown thinner than Bible paper and I was praying to Jesus Christ that it wouldn't rip.

Assistant: So. Working on any new videos?

Me: Nope, just trying not to die of humiliation at the moment.

Assistant: Is this your first physical?

Me: Ya. The closest I've ever had to a physical was my mom cleaning out my dick cheese when I was twelve.

Assistant: She did that until you were twelve?

Me: So, who is the doctor? Is he nice?

Assistant: It's a she and she's awesome! I showed her some of your videos last week during our lunch break! She loved them!

OH. MY. GOD. THIS. ISN'T. HAPPENING. GOD. DOESNT. EXIST.

Me: Oh really? Wow . . . that's cool.

Assistant: Ya! I told the whole office you were here! They are all so excited! We love when you put on that wig and act all ghetto!

I. CAN'T. STOP. SWEATING. I. WANT. TO. DIE.

Me: Awesome!

Assistant: Alright, I'll go get the doctor. Don't go anywhere!

Me: I won't!

I'M. GOING. TO. JUMP. OUT. THE. MOTHER. FUCKING. WINDOW.

The door opened and in walked the doctor. "She seems normal enough," said my brain in disturbing denial. "I'm sure she doesn't remember me at all! She must be fifty years old! Maybe she has a bad memory! Maybe she got amnesia on the way to the office today!"

Doctor: Hey! Where's your wig! I didn't recognize you!!

She laughed hysterically. My anus clenched.

Doctor: I'm kidding! How are you?

Me: I'm ok. Just ready to get this over with.

Doctor: Me too. You know how many balls I've touched today? More than all the Jonas brothers put together! HEYO!

She went for a high five. My anus clenched.

Doctor: Sorry, just trying to keep up with you, you crazy guy! So, let's get this started, shall we?

She walked up to me and asked me to lie down. As I lay down I looked at the ceiling and envisioned my head getting cut off by the ceiling fan. Anything to get my mind off the current situation. She reached her hand up my gown and grabbed my balls. She was gentle and polite about it. I closed my eyes and just let it happen. Things were going pretty smoothly until . . .

Doctor: Hey. Do Shananay.

That was the moment I knew my life would never be the same. I was no longer just a stranger getting his balls fondled by a doctor. I was a YouTube guy getting his balls fondled by a doctor who wanted him to tell offensive jokes in a ghetto woman's voice.

From that point on it only got crazier. Over the next seven years I would be stopped for pictures while I was peeing in a urinal, while I was vomiting outside of a theme park roller coaster, even while on the side of the road after I got into a car accident. But I would also learn how to handle it all surprisingly well. Nowadays, I never take it for granted, and I know that if it wasn't for people watching my videos I wouldn't be able to do any of the amazing things I've been able to do in the last several years.

The most insane situation was the first VidCon in 2010. For those who don't know, VidCon is a convention for You-Tubers to come together and meet their audiences. It now has over thirty thousand guests every year, but back in 2010 attendance was only a tenth of that. I was invited as a special guest and couldn't wait to meet the people who had been supporting me. I put on my ugliest vest, which I thought was fashion-forward, and headed to the convention center. During the drive over, I got a call from one of the people working at VidCon, who sounded like he was in crisis mode.

VidCon Worker: Shane?! WHERE ARE YOU??

Shane: On my way. What's going on?

VidCon Worker: Did you tweet that you were on your way??

Shane: Yes. Is that ok?

VidCon Worker: NO! There's a riot at the front door!

Shane: A riot? Come on, it can't be that bad.

I heard a scream in the background and I'm pretty sure I heard "I CAN'T FEEL MY LEGS!" but I could have been mistaken.

Shane: Oh my God!

VidCon Worker: When you get here we have three security guards. Text me when you are out front and we will assign them to you.

Three security guards?? I'm a YouTuber, not Obama! I make dumb videos on the internet and teach kids about sex. Why was I getting treated like a famous person? It made no sense to me and I was super uncomfortable. I guess I never felt worth that kind of attention; I still don't. But enough of my self-hatred, let's get back to the story. So I pulled up to the entrance and saw a crowd of over a thousand kids freaking out and knocking each other over. Some of them were holding signs with my name on them and others were wearing shirts with my face on them. Seeing my face plastered on a bunch of underage girls' chests was definitely not something I ever thought would happen. Just like I never expected my actual face would ever be on an of-age girl's chest in my life. I had a lot of emotions flowing through me, and I had an instant panic attack. As I stepped out of the car I was surrounded by teenagers. Three bodyguards walked up and took me by the arms. They escorted me through the crowd, and to say I looked like a douchebag is an understatement. I was a YouTuber surrounded by bodyguards. It doesn't get any douchier than that.

Luckily I was led to an area in the convention center where I got to do a meet-and-greet with the fans, and I met every single one of them. I stood there for eight hours hugging, taking selfies, signing mothers' boobs, and just having conversations with them about what was going on in their lives. It was amazing. It was at that moment that I didn't want to be invisible anymore. I felt like I was really making a difference in these kids' lives, and because of my videos some of them were able to have a happy escape. It was a magical day, and I will never forget it.

Which leads me back to the shitty Mexican restaurant on a Saturday night not so long ago. As I was leaving, my body decided that I needed to release all that questionable meat, and I needed to release it NOW. I ran to the bathroom, but it was locked, so I stood and waited while GRIPPING my

LOUD stomach. A family at a nearby table made eye contact and each had that same familiar "just saw a leprechaun" face. I prayed that they wouldn't come up to me, because at any moment my stomach was going to make butt gravy and I did NOT want them to smell what I was cooking. But it was too late; the leprechaun had been spotted. The family ran up to me and surrounded me by the bathroom. It was a mom holding a baby, two twelve-year-old kids, and a grandma. They were all speaking at once and asking for a shit-ton of selfies. I took pictures with the baby and the mama, the baby mama, and just the baby. At one point I'm pretty sure I was sitting on the grandma's lap while she was in her wheelchair. It got weird.

Then the bathroom door opened, so I politely told them good-bye, but to them "good-bye" meant "Let's go in the bathroom and watch him poop!" They all crowded into the small bathroom with me and started asking for advice on how to get popular on Instagram and if I'm friends with PewDiePie. I was trying to answer all their questions, but I had some of my own "PewDiePie" to make, so I tried my hardest to hint that I was ready for them to leave. Then a waitress walked in. I was relieved because I thought for sure she was going to tell them to get out and possibly give me some kind of free taco gift card. Instead she screamed . . .

Waitress: HEY! DO SHANANAY!

I now was in a single-person bathroom with an entire family and half the crew of the restaurant. Yet, I was still grateful and enjoyed how excited they were, until one of the twelve-year-olds hit me with a truth bomb.

Twelve-Year-Old: I thought you would be hotter in person. You're kinda ugly. LOL.

I don't know what was more offensive, the fact that she called me ugly or the fact that she used "LOL" in her everyday language. Either way, I wanted to be invisible. It was the first time since I was young that I had that feeling of wishing I could dissolve into the background. It's like she reached into my bean-filled body and ripped out my soul with her hand and crushed it. I went home after that and lay in bed for a good few hours and cried. I cried hard. I hadn't cried like that since Taco Bell came up with that Dorito taco thing. Except there was no happiness in my tears, just heartache. I considered taking a break from YouTube. The thought of going out in public and possibly seeing a fan made my heart shrivel up. What if they thought I was ugly too? What if every fan that has ever met me went back home and told their friends, "OMG, I had no idea Shane Dawson was DEFORMED! LOL!!"

I called my girlfriend, Lisa, and she calmed me down and talked me off the ledge.

Lisa: I know it hurts but just remember that's one person. There are millions of people who love you and if they saw you in public they would be so happy that they wouldn't even notice how ugly you are.

Shane: Gee . . . Thanks.

Lisa: I'm kidding. You aren't ugly. You're the sweetest, most beautiful guy in the world and there are so many people out there who agree with me. That girl was young and probably so nervous that she just blurted out something stupid. Please don't let it affect you.

Shane: I know. It's just hard.

Lisa: Remember all the kids you met at VidCon?

Shane: Ya.

Lisa: Did any of them call you ugly?

Shane: No . . . I guess not.

Lisa: Because they all love you so much. You are like a friend to them, or a creepy but loving older brother, and if you stopped making videos it would break their hearts. They would feel worse than you are feeling right now. Remember that.

And I did. The next day I woke up, showered, tried to make myself look less ugly, and filmed a video. I never want to go back to being invisible even if it means having to deal with the occasional person saying something rude to me. It's worth it. But you know what's not worth it? Eating at a Mexican restaurant that has a "C" rating on the window. Trust me. NOT WORTH IT.

HOW TO SURVIVE A
HORROR MOVIE

ABOUT THE ARTIST

America Valencia *took a drafting class in ninth grade and has been hooked ever since. She went on to study art and architectural design at the Art Institute of California. She is twenty-two years old and grew up in the Los Angeles neighborhood of Reseda, but currently resides nearby in Palmdale as a landscape and pool designer for CLD Designs.*

When I was a kid I would run around my house with a knife and pretend to murder my family. I know this sounds like something you might hear in a recording of a serial killer's therapy session, but I promise it's not that bad. I've had an obsession with horror films since I was around five years old. One day, I walked into the living room while my older brother was watching a movie called *Child's Play*. It was about a kid whose doll tried to kill him, which I found perfectly plausible because of all the terrible things I forced my dolls to do. I wouldn't have been surprised if they had eventually turned on me. Ask Furby. Actually, don't bother. I took out his batteries ages ago so he would keep his fucking mouth shut.

Anyways, my obsession with horror only grew when I saw the movie *Scream* a few years later. From the first scene, when Drew Barrymore gets hacked into pieces and hung on a tree in front of her parents' house, I was addicted. There's something so satisfying about watching a fictional character getting ripped to pieces and splattered all over the walls. I'm sure this says something about me as a person and my mental state, but whatever. I like what I like, and what I like is the sound of a knife scraping bone beneath the skin. Sue me!

Every time my friends would come over I would force

them to play "the *Scream* game." Basically it was me chasing them with a knife and them having to defend themselves with whatever household items were around. The only rules were that we couldn't actually hurt each other and whoever was the killer couldn't take off the mask, because if you took off the mask then it was just a kid running around trying to stab his friends, and even we knew that was too creepy.

Around age twelve I made my first short film, and it was more disturbing than any scary movie you've ever seen. It was basically me naked in a bathtub full of ketchup choking to death on my own ketchup blood. I'm not sure what the plot was, but it definitely had a twist ending. And by "twist ending" I mean it actually wasn't filmed by a creepy uncle in a dark basement.

I think the reason I became so obsessed with watching people die in movies is because it was a way for me to feel in control. I had very little control over my life as a kid and there was so much chaos and turmoil around me. My parents were always fighting and we had a lot of financial struggles. Watching horror films was a way for me to escape that and watch people who had even shittier lives than me. And to have a shittier life meant you had to be getting butchered by a seven-foot-tall monster with knives for fingers.

Another attempt at control was to hold in my poop. I would hold it in for days. So much so that when I burped people would ask, "Who farted?"

Either way, my dream was to one day star in my own horror film in which I could run around and get chased by an underpaid actor wearing a mask holding a rubber knife. That day finally came on my twenty-third birthday.

One of my good friends Michael Gallagher called me up and said he was directing a horror film called *Smiley* and he wanted me to be in it. Before he could even describe the plot I was already a thousand percent in. I could already picture myself covered in blood screaming for my life. I could also picture how many memes of me getting killed were going to be made by my haters. I was PUMPED! He sent me the script and it was a movie about a girl who gets stalked online by a killer who wears a mask with a smiley face carved into it. Not only did I have an epic death scene but I also got to play the killer! TWIST ENDING! This time without homemade child pornography! SCORE!

I showed up to the first rehearsal and met a couple of the other actors. It was the first time I had really acted in something other than YouTube sketches, so I was pretty nervous. I had stalked all of them on IMDb the night before and was immediately intimidated by what I found. They had all been in movies and TV shows, and some had been acting since they were kids. Which meant that while I was running around chasing my friends with a knife in some shitty house in Long Beach, they were on some set in Hollywood eating craft service and trying to divorce their parents! They had the life we normal people only dream about. Most of them were actually really nice.

My first scene was with the lead girl, who played my love interest. Having to act in love with someone you just met is incredibly awkward, especially when you just scarfed down a triple-layer burrito in the backseat of your car fifteen minutes earlier and your breath smells like bean farts. Luckily we decided to save the kiss until we got on set a few days later. That gave me plenty of time to get my mouth ready. I wanted it to be perfect for her. Not because I wanted her to fall in love with me or anything but because I didn't want her to go on Twitter afterward and say, "OMG just kissed @shanedawson and he tasted like Chipotle diarrhea!" So for the next few days I ate two packs of mints a day, wore four coatings of ultra-glossy ChapStick, and brushed my teeth in the morning and at night. That last one was the most challenging for me. Up until a year ago I didn't even know that brushing your teeth twice a day was the social norm! My philosophy was once in the morning and that's it! Why would you do it before bed? Who are you trying to get all fancy for? It's sleep, not prom!

The first week of production was great. I ate mass amounts of craft service, didn't fuck up my lines, and was even taught by a sassy extra how to twerk upside down with my feet against a wall. It was everything I had dreamed of as a kid, except for that twerking part. That wasn't a thing back then, but if it was you better bet my ass would have been twerking all over my house naked and covered in ketchup.

Everything was going great up until the last day of the shoot. I should have known it was going to be rough considering I'd had like five rape dreams in a row the night before, and I usually only have two. I also had some serious backne going on, and I know backne doesn't sound like a big deal but when you love popping zits as much as I do and you have a cluster of ready-to-go white-heads chilling in an unreachable part of your back, it's a nightmare. I used every item in my house I could find to try to pop them. At one point I had a pair of scissors taped to a Swiffer. I shoved the Swiffer between my mattress and box spring, got in a squat position, and leaned back. Unfortunately that just left me with numerous cuts and a really bloody Swiffer. Needless to say, as I walked up to the set that day I already felt off-kilter.

Since this was the first day we were shooting in a house, we had trailers set up outside. I was super pumped because I had never been inside one before. I had heard stories of actors having sex and popping painkillers, and I was excited to do the exact opposite. I was planning on falling asleep and possibly giving myself an over-the-jeans handy. What can I say, I'm a tease. But as I walked into my trailer I was stopped by a producer and was told that unfortunately there was a problem and I wouldn't be able to stay there. My first thought was, "Who clogged the toilet?" My second thought was, "For once it wasn't ME who clogged the toilet! Awesome!" But then as I walked away I noticed another actor walking into my trailer and closing the door.

Me: Does he know the toilet's clogged? Should we tell him? He looks like he eats a lot of kale so I'm assuming he's only gonna make matters worse.

Producer: The toilet isn't clogged.

Me: Oh . . . then why am I not in there? Is this because you think I'm gonna do something nasty in there? Because I promise, it's only above the jeans.

Producer: No, it's because that actor requested a trailer and it was the last one left.

Me: But . . . it was mine. It had a sign with my name on it. Granted, it was spelled wrong and I'm pretty sure someone extinguished their cigarette on it, but it was still mine.

Producer: He is being kind of a diva. He said he would call his agent if he didn't get the trailer. Would you mind doing us a solid and just letting him have it?

Me: Do I have a choice?

The producer looked at me with a "not really" look that reminded me of when I used to visit the school nurse and ask if I was in my healthy weight range. So I sucked it up and headed inside the house. He told me that there was a room where I could hang out. He pointed to a door that had a DON'T LET THE CATS OUT! sign on it. Purrfect. But I'm not a diva, so I threw my stuff down on some cats and whipped out my phone to look up this actor's Twitter to see how many followers he had. I saw that he had less than a thousand and I had a million. That gave me a good few minutes of shallow but necessary joy. I also loved that he gave his fans a pet name yet every tweet that he would send out to them had zero likes or retweets. It felt like a little gift from Jesus. Anyway, the first scene was coming up, and it was the one I had been waiting for, the big kiss. I hoped she wasn't allergic to cats.

My friend the director walked up to me with the girl playing my love interest and let us know how it was going to go down.

Director: Ok, so you guys are going to slowly kiss and then
    make your way to the bed.
Love Interest: Cool.
Me: Cool.

This seemed to be going well! Just two professional actors about to make out on camera in front of a hundred fat
dudes holding up lights and holding in their farts. Totally
easy! Everything was going great until another actress playing the part of my love interest's best friend walked over and
grabbed her away from me. They walked to the other side of
the room and looked like they were getting into some kind
of intense conversation. You would have thought they were
actually best friends, not just playing them in some horror
movie. Me being the nosiest person in the world, I decided
to walk past them and completely eavesdrop on the convo.

BFF: Don't do anything you aren't comfortable with.
Love Interest: What do you mean?
BFF: I've done plenty of love scenes before and the guy
    ALWAYS tries to shove his tongue down my throat.
    One guy even flicked my nipple.
Love Interest: What? Why?
BFF: I don't know. I guess nipple flicking is a thing in Japan.
    It was a foreign movie. Anyway, the point is, don't let
    him do anything to you.
Love Interest: I don't think he's going to. He seems sweet.
BFF: So do the Japanese. Tell that to my nipple.

I was PISSED. How could this random actress who had never even spoken to me assume that I was some kind of pervert who was trying to fuck my costar? If anything I just wanted to do my job as quickly as possible and go home so I could finish my binge session of some terrible reality show about a family who has a worse life than me.

So as we got ready to do the scene I noticed the crazy actress standing next to the camera, staring at my love interest with "DON'T WORRY I'M RIGHT HERE" eyes. I felt like I was about to make out with a girl while her overprotective mom watched. It was incredibly creepy, and because of my mommy issues, slightly a turn-on. ACTION. We went in for the kiss, and to say it was the worst kiss I've ever had would be an understatement. I've had better kisses from my gay uncle, and he likes to use tongue. CUT! The director pulled us aside.

> Director: That was great! Let's do it one more time but this time less like Amish kids experimenting with their siblings.

So we tried again and it somehow got worse. We did it about five times and then the director took us aside again. As we walked away I looked over at the crazy actress, and she was giving my love interest a thumbs-up. A THUMBS-UP? For what? For the most incestuous love scene ever put on film legally?

Director: This isn't working. The kiss is giving me goose
bumps. And not in a good way. In an "I just found out
my dad likes butt play" way.

Love Interest: Why are you looking at me?

Director: I'm not. I'm looking at both of you.

Love Interest: No you aren't. Just me.

Director: Ok, it's looking a little forced on your end. Is everything ok?

Me: Am I doing something to make you uncomfortable? I
swear I don't have a boner. This is just how my pants
look when I sit.

Love Interest: No, it's fine. Let's do it again.

She walked back to the bed and I stayed around to talk to
the director more.

Me: I think the other actress is getting in her head. She
told her I would flick her clitoris or something.

Director: What?

Me: I don't know, some Chinese guy in some movie stuck his
finger in her butt or something. I don't remember specifics.

Director: Well just try to make her comfortable. Be charm-
ing! Be you!

Me: Have you met me?

So I walked back over and sat on the bed next to my terrified lover.

Me: So ... see any movies lately?

Love Interest: No. You?

Me: I watched a documentary last night about these kids
    who killed their parents and then had sex in their beds.

Smooth. The director called action one last time and we
went for it. It was SLIGHTLY better but still felt like I was forcing my comatose sister to make out with me. Then the crazy
actress screamed out ...

BFF: OK! You guys got it!

She grabbed my love interest and took her off set.

Me: Dude. What the fuck was that?

Director: The best we're going to get.

Me: No, I'm talking about the insane actress with the crazy-
    people eyes and Adderall breath.

Director: You forgot all the IMDb credits.

Me: Fucking IMDb.

After that I went home and thought about how horrible
the kiss was. I couldn't stop thinking about it. A few weeks
later I got to see my love interest at an ADR session. "ADR"
stands for "automated dialogue replacement," which is used
when you have to record your voice and add it to the movie.
Usually because the microphone wasn't working on set. We
talked about the awkward kissing situation and she told me

about how nervous she had been to kiss on camera. It was her first time, so I totally understood where she was coming from. She also said it didn't help that the crazy actress girl was trying to act like a big sister and keep her safe from all the big mean rapist actors on set. I'm not sure what gave that girl the impression that I was a rapey perv, but honestly, I was just happy she didn't assume I was gay like every other stranger I meet daily.

The coolest part about the whole experience is that one day when I have my own kid I can show them their first scary movie ever and it will be one that their daddy was in. I'll just skip the make-out scene. I don't want them to think that's what kissing looks like. I'll just show them some porn for that.

THE MEAN GIRL GOT FAT

ABOUT THE ARTIST

Arturo André Jiménez *is a teenager with a quiet and warm spirit. He has loved drawing since he was in kindergarten. Being born near the border of the United States and Mexico has given him a unique perspective, and he looks forward to making his own path in life. He has received several honors and is currently working on a drawing for his local hospital. You can find some of his work on his Facebook page at https://www.facebook.com/AAJMART.*

You know when you're watching a terrible sitcom and something completely unrealistic happens to the main character and you are forced to suspend all disbelief until the show is over? Actually, that's every sitcom episode ever made. One day I lived out one of my childhood fantasies and got to be the lead character in the shittiest sitcom ever created: my life.

It started as a pretty typical day. I got up two hours early to straighten my embarrassingly long hair. I needed it to look extra stylish in preparation for my new position. I worked at a weight-loss center, and I had been promoted from a counselor to a salesperson. The difference was that when you were a counselor you would weigh the client and offer a little bit of wisdom. When you were a salesperson you would introduce them to the program and beg them to give you their money and then hand them off to someone else to deal with. It may sound like salesperson would have been an uncomfortable job, but being a counselor was way more uncomfortable, considering most clients liked to take off all their clothes at the scale and give you a big, naked hug if they'd lost a pound. Knowing that today I wasn't going to have to hug another naked, frizzy-haired soccer mom while some Kenny G song played on the lobby sound system made my life feel so much more worth living. I finished my hair, got into my tiny car, and practiced my sales pitch while driving to work.

As I walked into the center I was assaulted by my coworker Mag. She threw me into her office and locked the door.

Me: Mag, what's going on?!

Mag: Nothin'. Want a donut? They're filled.

Me: You dragged me in here for a donut?

Mag: No. I dragged you in here for a FILLED donut.

This wasn't odd behavior for Mag. She was a loud, outrageous, hilariously outspoken old Jew with a thick New Jersey accent and enough perfume to cover up the scent of a dead body rotting in her basement. Which, by the way, is the reason she gave me for why she wore so much perfume. She was also a cancer survivor and would tell you so every chance she got. Sometimes when a client would complain about gaining a pound she would tell them, "At least you have both your breasts. I have to draw on my second nipple with an eyebrow pencil." She really knew how to give her clients some perspective.

Me: No thanks. I gave up donuts a while ago.

Mag: Come on! Live a little! You know what happens when guys cut out sugar?

Me: They lose weight?

Mag: Ya, and they murder their wives and children. I heard about it on *Dr. Oz*.

Me: Well I'm not married and I have no kids, so I'll take my chances.

Mag: So, you nervous about your first day as a salesman? Listen, if they don't give you their money, take down their information and steal their identity. There's nothing like taking a "me" day at the spa and pretending to be some bitch you hate.

Me: You do that?

Mag: You a cop? Why are you asking so many questions?

Me: I just don't want to mess up. This is a big deal, ya know?

Mag: Honey, if you mess up you can just dust yourself off and try again. It's like I tell my clients: if you gained weight this week just go home, have yourself a good cry and a donut, and start over tomorrow.

Me: You tell your clients to eat donuts?

Mag: Of course! Your body needs sugar! It's like air but FILLED!

Me: How many of your clients have actually lost all their weight?

Mag: Um . . . none. Donut?

Mag wasn't the best counselor—hell, she was the worst—but she made up for it with her spirit. She probably should have been fired for not getting her clients to lose weight but they loved coming in to see her so much that it didn't really matter. It was a business, after all, and the bosses didn't really care about weight loss. They just wanted customers to keep coming back. So I walked out of Mag's office and into the lobby, where I saw an overweight young woman sitting nervously reading a magazine. I hadn't seen her before so I knew she was a new customer. The first thing I had been trained to do when a new customer came in was to greet them and hand them a health sheet to fill out. So I grabbed one, took a deep breath, and walked up to my first potential sale.

Me: Hi there. My name is Shane. What's your name?
Girl: Lacy.

As she took the health sheet out of my hand we locked eyes. I turned white as a ghost. I knew Lacy. I instantly had a flashback to two years prior when I was sitting in my high school biology class passing back a stack of tests to the girl behind me. It was Lacy. She was thin, beautiful, and everything that terrified me about women. She was a cheerleader with a 4.0 grade point average and more sexual experience then the sex ed teacher. One time she corrected him because he said the vagina only had three inches of feeling and she had proof it was nine. She was a mean girl in every sense of the word. Every day she would ask me questions about my outfit or my appearance. Not because she was curious, but because she was trying to make her horrible friends laugh. Here's a sample conversation from 2006:

Lacy: Where did you get that shirt? It's SUPER sexy.
Me: Um . . . Walmart I think.
Lacy: WOW. Really? I never would have guessed that! I love

the way it highlights your back muscles. How often do you go to the gym to get back muscles like that? You must have a six-pack back there.

I didn't have back muscles. The bitch was referring to the rolls of fat that were squished underneath my shirt between my shoulder blades and my ass. She was a soulless demon monster and she was now sitting before me, three hundred pounds, and potentially my first sale.

Me: Fill this out. I'll be right back!

I casually ran to my office and slammed the door. I started hyperventilating into a brown lunch bag like a cartoon character having a panic attack. Mag walked into the room and tried to calm me down.

Mag: What's going on? Here! Have some casserole.

I was too panicked to ask how she had managed to procure a vat of piping-hot casserole with no oven in sight, only a disgusting, decades-old microwave stuck in a dusty corner of the employees' break room. All I could think about was how my ex–high school enemy was sitting one hundred feet away from me.

Me: That girl out there—
Mag: Oh ya, saw her at the donut shop earlier. Bitch took all the jellies.

Me: She's . . . she's . . .

Mag: Spit it out! I got shit to do! Oprah's on in five minutes and she's interviewing a woman whose face was ripped off by an ape! I only have four minutes and fifty-nine seconds to finish my casserole.

Me: That girl made my life hell in high school.

Mag: What did she do? Swoop up all the tater tots in the cafeteria before you could?

Me: No! She was the skinny hot cheerleader who reminded me how fat I was every day!

Mag: She was a hot cheerleader? Wow. Did she eat the mascot?

Me: I don't know what to do.

Mag: Did she recognize you?

Me: No.

Mag: Well then get revenge on that pom-pom-twirlin' cunt.

Me: What do you mean?

Mag: Sign her up, then give her to me as a client. I'll make sure she doesn't lose the weight. Hey, I can even get her fatter! I'll tell her that she should do the mayo-and-cream-cheese diet! It might even kill her!

Me: I don't know—

Mag: Ok, well you figure it out! I gotta go! Ape face is on!

I took a deep breath and walked back out to the lobby. Lacy had finished filling out her health sheet so I walked her back to the scale. We made small talk.

Me: So, what brings you in today?

Lacy: I just need to get off all this baby weight.

Baby weight?? She had a baby? The plot was thickening and this had just gone from a sitcom to a Diablo Cody movie. Except with less witty banter and more sad, fat tears.

Me: Does your husband know you're here?

Lacy: Oh, I don't have one.

Single parent at twenty? This had just gone from a Diablo Cody movie to an MTV reality show! Except with less weave snatching but the same number of sad, fat tears. As I turned on the scale she looked at it with fear in her eyes. I started feeling less intimidated by her. She wasn't the evil queen bee I hid from in high school. She was a sad girl who had been through a lot of hardship since then. I didn't quite know how to deal with this revelation. I wanted to cry but I also wanted to punch her in the face for calling me "Six-Pack Back Fat" for four years. But from the looks of it, life had already punched her in the face. And then kicked her while she was down. We went back to my office and sat down. She teared up, and I handed her a tissue.

Me: So, tell me a little bit about why you want to lose the weight.

Lacy: Well, after I found out I was pregnant I fell into a depression. I just started eating everything around me.

My boyfriend left when he found out about the baby. It's fine, he was an asshole anyways. I was only with him because he was the only guy I had ever been with in high school. I guess I was too scared to leave.

She was right. He was an asshole. Her boyfriend had been a football-playing douchebag and had also made my life miserable. One time he started a rumor that I had herpes. Not from sex, but from a dirty toilet seat that I sat on at a Del Taco. The sad part is that it's totally possible. I used a lot of toilets at a lot of Del Tacos. Sometimes your body can't wait till you get home.

Me: What made you want to lose the weight now?

Lacy: I'm tired of hiding. I haven't seen any of my friends for over a year because I don't want them to see me like this. I was scared to even come today because I thought maybe someone would recognize me. I usually just take care of the baby and ask my mom to go out and get groceries and stuff. I don't even remember the last time I did something fun on the weekend.

I wanted to tell Lacy who I was but I was afraid it would make her run away. So instead I listened and tried to explain to her how the weight-loss program worked. We talked for about an hour and it was time for me to assign her a counselor. Mag walked past the door of my office with a big smile on her face. She couldn't wait to get her evil hands on Lacy and fill her up like a human éclair. But I couldn't do that. I ended up giving her to a counselor who would actually help her lose weight. I walked Lacy out to her car. Before she got in, I broke the news to her.

Me: Lacy . . . I want to tell you something.
Lacy: Is everything ok?
Me: I'm Shane. From high school.

It took her a few moments but then it hit her like a truck full of mayo and cream cheese.

Lacy: Oh my God. Wow! You're skinny!
Me: Ya, thanks. I just wanted you to know that I'm not mad at you for how you treated me in high school.
Lacy: How did I treat you?
Me: The way I used to treat a toilet at Del Taco.
Lacy: Wow. That bad?
Me: Ya. You don't remember?
Lacy: Not really. I kind of blocked out those four years. High school was terrible. Every day I hoped I would get trampled to death by the school band.
Me: What? But you were popular! And hot!
Lacy: Thanks?
Me: I mean, not that you aren't hot now . . . I'm just saying. In high school your life was great.
Lacy: It's funny. Everybody always thinks that. I guess I put on quite a good act.
Me: Ya. I guess you did.

She reached out and hugged me. If Lacy from two years ago had known that one day she would be giving me a hug, I'm sure she would have vomited all over her pom-poms.

Lacy: I'm sorry I was such a bitch to you.
Me: It's ok. I guess we all hated high school, didn't we?
Lacy: Ya.

She got in her car and drove off. I was upset that she didn't remember how horribly she'd treated me, but I guess I never thought about her reasons for doing so. She must have been dealing with a lot of issues that made her take out her anger on me. It doesn't make it right but it makes it slightly understandable. Either way, I'd just had my first successful sale on my first day as a salesperson and I felt seriously accomplished. I walked right into Mag's office and sat down next to her.

Mag: You want a donut?
Me: Hell ya.

MY GIRL (SPACE) FRIENDS

ABOUT THE ARTIST

Michaela Larson *is a sophomore in high school. She has always loved art and takes classes every chance she gets.*

'm not really what most would consider a "manly man." Hell, I don't even really consider myself a "man" at all. I'm more of a "woman with man parts." Kind of like that scene in *Toy Story* where that asshole kid made a toy out of Barbie's torso and GI Joe's limbs. I'm pretty sure that's how God made me. He probably had an "oops" pile full of body parts and decided to throw them all together and make a human gumbo. Because my brain and heart skew more feminine, I was always surrounded by girl friends. Yes, that space was intentional. I never had a "girlfriend" until I was in my early twenties, but up until then I had an ever-changing collection of "girl (SPACE) friends."

I met my first girl (SPACE) friend when I was six years old, and her name was Kaley. We lived a few houses apart from each other and hung out pretty much every day after school. We had very similar interests, like playing with Barbies, watching *Mrs. Doubtfire* on a loop, and peeing the bed. Ok, that last one was just me. But she didn't judge me for it. When I would sleep over at her house her mom would give me a rubber sheet to tuck into my sleeping bag, turning it into a human-sized condom. It wasn't the most comfortable thing in the world but it was better than completely destroying their living room carpet. We were friends up until I was about ten. I'm not really sure what happened or why we drifted apart but I do remember a bizarre incident during which I punched her in the vagina to see if it hurt as bad as getting punched in the balls. That little experiment MIGHT have caused her to rethink our friendship. Understandable.

I met my next girl (SPACE) friend when I was eleven years old, and her name was Sara. She was a little more experimental than Kaley, which is why I think we got along. A punch to the vagina was never out of the question. I'm pretty sure she even let me finger her once. It wasn't sexual at all. It was more just to see what was in there. I was CONVINCED that women had hidden jewels inside of them. Call me a pussy pirate. But our friendship wasn't just about discovering each other's bodies, it was also about discovering each other's mental issues. I'm pretty sure she was schizophrenic and I'm pretty sure I was a pathological liar. Her imaginary friends were WAY too detailed and at one point I told her that I was actually an alien from another planet. And I believed it. Neither of us sought psychiatric counseling, but we played doctor a lot, so that balances everything out, right? We ended our friendship because I moved across town, and long-distance friendships don't really work when you're eleven. This was pre-internet, so we didn't have Twitter to follow each other on. It was almost like she'd died, and I totally forgot about her. Wow.

Through the next fifteen years I had many more girl (SPACE) friends. They were all different and unique in their own ways. Some of them were crazy, some were adventurous, some were in wheelchairs, but they all shared one trait: they were nonjudgmental. I can't stand judgmental people. The second somebody lifts their eyebrow at a situation I cut them out of my life. I like to live in a world where people can be whoever the fuck they want to be and say whatever the fuck they want to say. It's interesting to me, entertaining even. I'm a glorified people watcher. And there's nothing better than sitting back—no judgment of course—and watching people be themselves. It's like TV but with no commercials, like a movie but with no annoying "turn off your phone" ads, like a play but . . . eh, never mind. I kinda fuckin' hate plays. They're the worst. It's not judgmental to say that, right? Oh well, already said it. Can't take it back.

The one girl (SPACE) friend who has lasted the longest is Kate. We met when we were in sixth grade and bonded over the fact that we were both total fucking losers. That's usually how I bond with people, over a realization that we are both lame and need each other. Probably not the healthiest way to start a friendship, but hey, what friendships are really all that "healthy" anyways? My friendships are usually big bags of fattening potato chips with a big jar of processed cheese on the side for dippin'. Finger-lickingly unhealthy. Anyways, we stayed friends throughout middle school and high school and she's the only friend from the past I still see on a weekly basis. We lost touch slightly in high school, mainly because we both got boobs over the summer after eighth grade. Hers got her a few new cool friends and mine kept me in the loser circle.

Kate has seen me at my worst, my best, and at my (pretty

much all the time) mediocre. They say friendships between boys and girls always turn romantic no matter how hard you try to fight it. Those people are whores with no self-control. Wow. That was pretty judgmental of me. Ok, let me backtrack.

I'm not going to lie; there was a moment in time when Kate and I dipped our toes into the cold, frigid, unsanitary lake of "more than friends," but it lasted literally two hours. I remember those two hours vividly. I was eighteen and I picked her up from her house on a Friday night like I always did. I'd just had my car washed because the night before I'd hit some kind of animal on the freeway. To this day, I tell myself it was an opossum so I can sleep at night. It was definitely a puppy. Most likely a rescue. Most likely owned by a child who NEEDED it. Anyways, I honked my horn and she ran out of her house to my car like someone just blew a starting air horn at a marathon. I'm not exactly sure what was going on in her house, but it must have been pretty bad for her to bolt out like that. I'm assuming a family game of Monopoly or worse . . . YAHTZEE. I actually shivered as I typed that. So she got into my car and we went off to have one of our weekly adventures. These usually consisted of trips to the mall, maybe a dinner at Denny's, sometimes a movie, and always ended with hours of watching YouTube videos of people falling down and/or having fatal accidents. Our favorite was a video of a baby getting hit by a bus. I promise, it was WAY funnier than it sounds.

At dinner we had a moment. Not like in the movies where two friends look at each other and see "more." And then they kiss each other in the rain and say things through their happy tears like, "I can't believe it took me this long to realize this," or "It's always been you." It wasn't like that at all. It was more of an "I guess if we wanted to date each other we could. Like . . . it would be pretty easy and convenient. We see each other ALL the time. I mean, we're practically married anyways." See? Not that romantic.

The thought wasn't totally random though. A waitress came over and said, "Aww, you guys are a cute couple." We didn't say anything. We didn't deny it. We didn't say thank you. We just sat there. We looked at each other with "Eh . . . I guess, maybe?" in our eyes. We talked it out over a huge basket of sweet potato fries and milkshakes. Once again, I wasn't exaggerating when I said my friendships were unhealthy. "So . . . should we date?" I said through my mouth full of greasy mush.

"I dunno . . . ," she said with a huge drip of milkshake going from her mouth to her shirt. And then the conversation went a little something like this.

Me: I mean, aren't we kind of already dating?
Her: I guess. My parents think we are. They also think I'm a lesbian and that you're gay.
Me: Cool. I like your parents.
Her: They're ok I guess.

Chewing. Swallowing. Sipping.

Me: So . . . should we go on a real date?

Her: Ok. Isn't that just dinner and a movie? We kind of already did that tonight.

Me: Well if I would have known it was a date I would have put on deodorant and not talked about trimming my ball hair for the first time.

Her: I can't believe you used your mom's mustache scissors to do that.

Me: Ya. I hope she doesn't find out.

More chewing. More swallowing. More sipping. Silence.

Her: I don't want to stop talking about your ball hair. Or stop telling you about my weird growths on my body.

Me: Me neither. Well, the ball-hair thing. You can really stop talking about the growths. I get it, you have melanoma. Don't rub it in my face.

Laughter. Chewing. Staring.

Her: Friends?

Me: Ya. Friends.

Smiling. Pause. Loud fart.

Me: I thought that would be quieter.

Her: Nope. Everyone heard it.

Me: Awesome. Check!

So after that we never talked about it again. We weren't meant for each other in "that way." We were meant for each other in a different way. She has become a member of my family, a sister of sorts. And to this day I can't imagine life without her. She is one of the only things in my life that is a constant, and I cherish that. So, Kate, if you're reading this, thank you for wanting to hear about my balls and not caring about my gassy stomach. But seriously, stop talking about your growths. Just go to the fucking doctor already.

MY STRANGE ADDICTIONS

ABOUT THE ARTIST

Leonie Lerner *is an artist and musician living in Port Washington, New York, where she attended high school. She has studied drawing, pottery, and classical piano, and is an avid photographer. Leonie is pursuing a career in arts and psychology. Her Twitter handle is @leonie_rl.*

The smell of death and bags of pee filled my nose as I laid in silence on a crunchy plastic sheet. I was nineteen and once again found myself in an emergency room hospital bed on a Sunday morning. I was used to this by now, considering I had been there at least six times already that year.

Before I get into why I treated the ER like a rich person's vacation home, I want to give you some backstory about an issue I've had my whole life. I'm addicted to everything. I know a lot of people say they have a "chocolate addiction" because they get an extra scoop of ice cream for dessert, or they have a "shoe addiction" because they have one too many pairs in their closet. I don't just get an extra scoop of rocky road or have one too many pairs of Skechers Shape-ups. (Yes, I actually own those. Don't judge me.) I am severely addicted to everything I see or touch that gives me some sense of joy. Luckily I'm not addicted to my Skechers Shape-ups. Those were murder on my calves and didn't give me the ass they promised in the commercial.

When I was a kid I became addicted to food, and not in the typical way kids do, but in a Hoover-vacuum-sucking-up-everything-in-its-path kind of way. I wouldn't just eat an Oreo, I would eat the whole box and then move on to something else.

I remember at one point running out of real food, so I started eating condiments and spices. You haven't lived till you've had ketchup pepper soup. Every time I would go to a friend's house I couldn't even focus on the games we were playing because I was thinking about what was in their kitchen. I had one friend who was always stocked up on name-brands like Pop-Tarts and Coca-Cola, unlike my house, which had Generic Brand Breakfast Bars and Dark Brown Drink. All I could think was, "Why are they not all eating right now? They have so much food! If I were them I would put a chair in front of the fridge and go at it! Preferably a chair with no armrests so I could fully let myself expand."

When my mom and I would take trips to the store she would have to drag me out of there because I would just stand in the aisle and stare at every single product. If I could have I would have eaten the entire store, clerks and baggers included. I'm not above cannibalism.

Another one of my addictions was friends. No, not the television show about a fictional New York City that has no black people in it. Actual friends. When I met someone I liked I would want to spend every second with them. They became my ketchup pepper soup, minus the stomach ulcers. I wanted to be at their house, hang out with their family, play with their dog, skin them alive, and wear them as a bodysuit. That last one might be an exaggeration but the thought did cross my mind a few times. Except I was way bigger than my friends, so I would have probably had to sew two friends together. Or maybe just wear their face as a mask? I've thought about this way too much.

Every year I would have a new friend because every year my current friend would become overwhelmed by my clinginess and stop hanging out with me. This is something that I still struggle with but to a lesser extent. When I start feeling myself becoming addicted to hanging out with someone I limit the amount of time I see them. I'm scared I will fall into old habits and start thinking about how good their flesh would feel on mine in that bloody skin suit.

When I was seventeen years old I had a pretty rough experience that made me want to lose all my weight and lose it fast. I was with all my friends at an amusement park and we were going to ride the newest extreme roller coaster. I hadn't ridden a roller coaster since I was a kid, so I was super pumped to get thrown around by a machine and then vomit into a trash can filled with cotton candy wrappers afterward. As I made my way onto the ride I realized that the seat belt wasn't big enough to go around my waist. I had a full-on panic attack. How could this be? I was fat but I wasn't "that fat." Well, turns out I was. One of the workers walked over and escorted me off the ride. All my friends watched as I burst into tears and was taken to the exit. That was one of the worst days of my life, and even thinking about it now makes me feel like vomiting into an amusement park trash can.

That experience sent me into overdrive. I lost 150 pounds in less than a year by eating nothing but chicken and doing nothing but running. I stopped hanging out with friends, and I stopped being able to have a normal conversation with anyone because all I wanted to talk about was weight loss and health. I literally became one of those annoying-ass clerks that you try to avoid at Whole Foods, except I wore deodorant.

While I was losing the weight I became addicted to something that was more harmful than any typical drug. I became addicted to the artificial sugar called Splenda.

Now, I know this is going to sound insane, and I'm sure you aren't going to fully believe me, but at my peak I was eating over 250 packets of Splenda a day. That's enough to last a normal person over a year. That's 250 times more than any human should consume, considering one of the ingredients in Splenda is the same ingredient used in pool-cleaning products. The addiction started when I was hanging out with a friend one day and she was sipping on an iced coffee.

> Me: God. I want something sweet so bad. You know how
>   long it's been since I had sugar?
> Friend: It's not worth it! You look so good now! What's
>   more important, eating ice cream or being able to see
>   your penis?
> Me: You're asking the wrong guy.
> Friend: Have you tried Splenda?
> Me: What's that?
> Friend: It's fake sugar. It's pretty good. Here, I have an extra
>   one I didn't use in my coffee.

So I opened it and gave it a taste. From that moment on, life had a brand-new meaning. How did I not know about this until now?! This was heaven in a small paper packet! If I could

I would have dumped out all the packets in Starbucks and made Splenda angels in the middle of the store! I started using Splenda in everything. I put it in my cereal, on my vegetables, in my iced tea, and even directly into my mouth. After two years or so I got up to two full boxes a day, which added up to about 250 packets. I started talking about it on my YouTube channel, and kids would send packets to my PO box. Boxes and boxes were kept stored in my powder-covered garage. It looked like I was involved in some kind of drug-smuggling operation. I even planned out my own funeral. Instead of dropping flowers into a six-foot-deep hole before burying me, I wanted my friends and family to drop in packets of Splenda with handwritten notes on them. (I like thinking about death a lot, another one of my addictions.)

The overdose of Splenda mixed with my unhealthy diet of chicken and vegetables (and nothing else) brought me to the hospital six times in one year. My life was on a downward spiral, and I couldn't get a grip on it. I was constantly passing out from dehydration and having intense panic attacks that my doctor believed were side effects from too much artificial sugar and way too much caffeine. My family was always concerned but there was nothing they could say to me to change my mind. I loved that sweet poison, and I didn't care about the side effects. At one point my skin even started to turn yellow, and not in a cute fake-tanner way, in a HOLY-SHIT-WHY-IS-THAT-GUY-YELLOW way. Which leads me to this specific trip to the ER, which changed everything.

It was a hot summer day in Florida, and my family and I

were hanging out at Disney World. I had never been there, so I was ready to see what all the hype was about. I was ready to ride some dumb rides and get stopped a million times for pictures by Japanese tourists who thought I was Zac Efron. I had my huge iced tea with fifty Splendas mixed in and was ready to take on the day. The thing about Florida that I wasn't aware of is that they have occasional summer rainstorms. My first thought was, "Oh my God, my hair. Now those Japanese tourists are going to mistake me for Vanessa Hudgens!" My second thought was, "Oh my God . . . humidity." I did NOT do well with humidity. Not only did I hate feeling sticky, but I was already constantly dehydrated, so when it got humid outside I would start to feel insanely light-headed. The rain started sprinkling and my hair started frizzing. I started having a panic attack because I could feel the hot Florida air entering my lungs and sucking out all the moisture. My heart started racing because I knew that soon I was going to pass out. Every time I had passed out in the past, it had been because I was overheated, and the last thing I wanted to do was pass out at Disney World and get trampled by people running to get a picture with a former convict wearing a *Monsters, Inc.* costume. I ran to the bathroom because I figured it would be air-conditioned. My brother followed me inside.

Brother: Dude, are you ok?
Me: I just need air. I need cold air.

The bathroom didn't have air-conditioning so he started splashing cold water from the sink on my face. This is when things began to get foggy, and I don't remember much of what happened next. I got so dehydrated that I went a little crazy and started acting like a child star having a breakdown in front of TMZ cameras. My brother told me later what happened, and it went a little something like this.

Me: I think the devil is in me!
Brother: What??
Me: He's in me!! I want him out!!!!

So I guess I took down my pants and hopped into the cold-water-filled sink and started screaming obscenities.

Me: GET HIM OUT OF ME!!! I'M GONNA SHIT HIM OUT!!!!

My mom rushed in and saw me having a total mental breakdown, so she called 911. The next thing I knew I was waking up in a hospital room with Disney characters all over the walls. I thought I was in hell. As I lay in the hospital bed I looked over and saw my mom asleep in the chair next to me. She looked so tired. Not just tired because it was early in the morning but tired because the constant trips back and forth to the hospital were wearing on her. I could see it in her face that all the emotional distress of seeing her son slowly die a fake-sugary death in front of her was taking its toll. The doctor walked in with a clipboard and a concerned look on his face.

Doctor: Hello, Shane.

Me: Hey. What's going on?

Doctor: So you had a little bit of an episode, didn't you?

Me: I don't remember. Oh God, did I kill someone? My mom always said I reminded her of one of those kids who could snap one day.

Doctor: No, you passed out. You were severely dehydrated, but don't worry, we are giving you lots of fluids.

Me: Oh. Ok, that's fine.

Doctor: Fine?

Me: Ya, it happens all the time. I pass out like once a month pretty much. The ER by my house and I are friends on MySpace.

Doctor: Why do you pass out? How is your diet?

Me: Um . . . not great.

Doctor: I'd like you to tell me. I want to understand what's going on here.

Me: Well . . . I eat ok. Chicken and veggies. It's the fake sugar that's kind of a situation.

Doctor: How much fake sugar are you eating?

Me: Two hundred fifty packets a day. Usually a couple gallons of iced tea. Sometimes a twelve-pack of diet soda.

The expression on his face will forever be burned on my brain. He looked like he was having a *That's So Raven* vision, but instead of seeing something funny between him and his kooky redheaded friend Chelsea, he was seeing me dead.

Me: I know. It's pretty bad.

Doctor: You need to get off that ASAP. It's extremely bad for you. How much water do you drink?

Me: I swallow some by accident when I brush my teeth?

Doctor: Shane, I'm going to share something with you that I haven't even told your family. When you came in here today you were so dehydrated that you were inches away from slipping into a coma. If you had waited a few more hours to come in you would probably be in one right now.

Me: Oh my God. Really?

Doctor: Your entire insides were drier than a potato chip. Your brain was malfunctioning, which is why you were sitting in a public sink trying to shit out the devil.

Me: WHAT?

Doctor: It's serious, Shane. Really, really serious.

That hit me hard. It wasn't just about me anymore, it was about everyone in my life. If I were to end up in a coma or, even worse, dead, it would affect so many people. The taste of that sweet sugary powder wasn't worth it anymore. I know the old saying "Nothing tastes as good as being thin feels." Well, nothing tastes as good as being alive either. From that moment forward I decided to get off the packet once and for all. But I want to be clear: it wasn't just the fake sugar that was causing me to go to the hospital. It was everything related to it. I was drinking gallons of iced tea every day because it tasted so good with Splenda in it. Iced tea is insanely dehydrating. Combine that with the fact that I hadn't had actual water in a year, and you get a recipe for coma. I also wasn't eating right and hadn't been for a long time. I would starve myself and then go on binges and eat crazy amounts of frozen yogurt and ranch dressing. Not together. I'm mentally sick but not that sick.

So I started changing my diet and got on a normal routine, but the road hasn't been easy. At twenty-six years old I still struggle every day with my addictions. All I want to do is get a big gallon of ice cream and lie in bed all day and watch Netflix, but I can't. I don't want my addictions to rule my life. This is a huge reason why I don't drink or do any kind of drugs. I can't imagine what my life would be like if I tried cocaine. I'm sure my house would be super clean and I'd be way funnier to hang out with, but the side effects wouldn't be worth it. I think one day I might be able to have just one packet of Splenda and be ok, or have just one drink and not turn into a raging alcoholic. But I'm not there yet. Right now I'm just living one daily vlog at a time.

Did I mention I'm addicted to YouTube?

YOUTUBE GOT ME FIRED

ABOUT THE ARTIST

Chloe Guillory *is a senior at Magnolia High School in Texas. She began drawing in the eighth grade and she comes from an artistic family. She is seventeen years old and draws as a hobby when she's not onstage performing in her high school's theater productions. You can find her on Instagram at @weridthatsme and on Twitter at @werido17.*

've always been a hardworking guy. It's actually one of my downfalls. Well, that and dipping sauces. I can really fuck up the condiments bar at a Fuddruckers. Waitresses always think I'm joking when I ask for a serving tray of different dipping-sauce options with my meal. They laugh and tell me how hilarious I am. I don't laugh and tell them to GET ME A TRAY OF SAUCES.

When I was seven my first job was getting the newspaper every morning from the front porch and taking it upstairs to my grandma. I know it sounds simple, but I was obese and my front porch had like six steps, so it was a daily struggle. Also the fact that I had to walk up another thirty steps to get to my grandma's bedroom made it damn near impossible. I saw a commercial for one of those electronic "stair chairs" for handi-capped people that literally lifts you from the first floor all the way up to the second story of the house. It was on my wish list to Santa every year. I never got it. But I did get a Princess Diana Beanie Baby in a glass box, so all is forgiven.

When I was twelve I moved on to bigger and better things. I sent in my letter of resignation to my grandma and told her that I needed to explore other options. There was more out there for me. More than just getting the paper every morning in exchange for a few fat-free SnackWell's cookies. I was going to be the richest kid on our block, which wasn't saying a lot considering the richest kid on our block still couldn't afford braces at fifteen. Poor kid looked like he'd taken a bite out of the street. I was going to be a success, and I was going to do it the American Way: make a bunch of shitty products and force my neighbors to buy them because they felt bad for me. I had a plethora of ideas. Some were better than others, but they all had one thing in common: they were terrible. One was a frozen ice-cream pop that was made from fat-free yogurt and peanut butter. It literally ripped off my taste buds and made my tongue bleed for two hours. But instead of adjusting the recipe to make it not tongue-bleedingly dangerous, I just decided to sell it the way it was. I sold about ten of them the first day, which was great, but shockingly I didn't get any reorders. So it was time to move on to my next product: friendship bracelets.

What do you need to show that you and your friend care about each other? Not open communication, not acceptance of each other's flaws. No no no. You need shitty-ass bracelets that are impossible to take off so you end up getting dirt, shit, and garbage all over them. Ya, that's what friendship is. I sold about fifteen of them and I felt like I'd struck gold. You should have heard my pitch. It usually went something like this:

[Ding dong]
Old Lady: Ooooh! Is it Girl Scout cookie season already?!
Me: No. I'm not a girl, and I don't have cookies.
Old Lady: Oh. Well that's unfortunate.
Me: But I do have something better!

Old Lady: Save it. I'm an atheist.

Me: I don't know what that word means. I'm twelve.

Old Lady: Well, by the looks of you and what "God" gave you to work with . . . you'll know the word pretty well in your teens.

Me: Looking forward to it. What I'm actually here about is a product I'm very excited to share with you! Tell me, do you have any friends?

Old Lady: They're all dead.

Me: Great! Well, wouldn't it be nice to have something to remember them by?

Old Lady: My last friend stole my husband, so . . . that's kind of hard to forget.

Me: Wow. That got dark really fast. Well, I have something more uplifting than a rage-filled vengeful heart! How about . . .

[Whips out shitty bracelets from a *Home Improvement* lunch box]

Me: Friendship bracelets!

Old Lady: Cute. I'm closing the door now. I have to change my colostomy bag. This experience has completely filled it.

Me: Please, hear me out, Mrs. . . . . I don't know your name so I'll just call you Mrs. Beautiful.

She blushed. Not sure if it was from flattery or embarrassment from the smell of her colostomy bag leaking, but either way, she was engaged.

Me: Now, who's somebody in your life that you can rely on?

Old Lady: My cat, Cheddar.

Me: Great! But let's try a human.

Silence.

Me: Mrs. Beautiful . . . Do you want to be my friend?

Old Lady: Not really.

Me: Ok. Then let's just be bracelet buddies.

I tied a bracelet on her wrist.

Me: Whenever you look down at this bracelet just remember that there's someone in the world wearing the same bracelet on the same wrist looking down at it too.

I tied a matching bracelet on my wrist.

Me: So whenever you look down, you won't feel alone. Kinda cool, right?

Old Lady: Yes. Yes it is.

She smiled. Adjusted her bracelet. Got it to the right fit. Looked back up at me.

Old Lady: You give that speech to all the lonely ladies on the block?

Me: I'm only wearing one bracelet, ma'am.

We shared a smile. She handed me five bucks. And I was on my way.

Now, I'm not gonna lie. I was playing with her emotions. I knew that she was lonely and that feeling like there was someone who cared might make her more inclined to buy something from me, but is that so bad? She was a sad old lady who smelled like feces and had a cat named after a type of government cheese. Who WOULDN'T feel bad for her? But that's what made me a great salesman. I CARED. Which led me to my next job, which was six years and a lot of hair product later: weight-loss products salesman.

I walked into the front door of a very prominent national weight-loss center in Huntington Beach, California, two days after my eighteenth birthday. I was ready for a "grown-up" job. Selling bracelets to old ladies isn't as cute when you are a teenager with constant accidental boners. I needed something with benefits and responsibilities. Something that I could be proud of. And to me, helping people shed pounds was perfect. Besides, I knew these people. These were *my* people. I could share all my experiences with them and show them there was a light at the end of the tunnel. If only the company had felt the same way. From what I could tell even on that first day on the job, its mission was to make as much money off fat people as possible.

For those of you who don't know how weight-loss management companies work, I'll break it down for you. Imagine a grocery store where the lady at the checkout counter asks you to reveal all your darkest demons and then gives you a smiley-face sticker and asks for your credit card. It's pretty much like that. Except in this case that lady at the checkout was an eighteen-year-old boy who had NO idea how to help people with their physiological problems and had no nutritional knowledge whatsoever. Before walking through the front door of the center I had to go through five days of "Nutrition 101," which sounds way more informative than it was. It was basically me and six other hopeful employees sitting in a creepy back room at some abandoned weight-loss center being lectured by a suicidal divorcée about the food pyramid. One of our topics of the day was "Things my ex-husband eats that make him a fat piece of shit." That one was pretty informative, actually.

After five days of that we got a certificate (which I'm pretty sure you could just find on Google Images and print out) and were given the go-ahead to "join the family." Sitting with a group of older women being told that we were now joining the "family" made the whole thing very *Sister Wives*. I was the gay-looking husband and they were my unattractive, annoying significant others who I secretly hoped would die in a house fire while I was at work.

The first thing I did before starting my new job was go to Target and get the fanciest first-day outfit I could find for $20 or less. I purchased ill-fitting black pants that showcased my white gym socks underneath, a faux silk button-up shirt that was NOT sweat resistant, and a two-sizes-too-tight Jonas Brothers vest that had "vanity buttons" on the shoulders. Looking back, I looked like a Claymation Tim Burton character. But at the time, I thought I was the shit. I even remember thinking, "If I ever win a Teen Choice Award I'm TOTALLY gonna rock this on the purple carpet!" Which happened, and I did. But that's another embarrassing story for another time. Back to fat pimping.

I walked into the weight-loss center, and to my surprise there was nobody there. It was creepy. Like an abandoned city in a zombie movie. All that was left were empty chairs with coats hanging off the backs and the lingering smell of cheese curls. After about ten minutes of looking around, I opened the back door and there they were, all the employees, smoking cigarettes, eating gyros from a truck, and having a burping contest. And the best part is they were doing all this while standing under a HUGE sign that said: LIVE HEALTHY. The irony was bigger than my "before" picture. It was practically busting out of its seams.

It was then I realized this whole company was a facade and it was just another way for America to make money off fat people. But I didn't hate the job. I ended up working there for over three years, and I became one of their most successful salespeople in the entire country. I would have bigwigs come up to me at conventions and ask, "How do you do it? How do you sell so much?!" And my response was simple: I care. I actually wanted to sell the clients the food and see them every week because I wanted them to succeed and lose the weight. But I also had a winning sales pitch to help me out when a new customer wasn't biting.

[Ding. The scale hits a high number. The new customer is in denial.]

Customer: That's not right. Maybe it's my shoes.

Me: It's not your shoes. Its time you take control of your life . . . today.

Customer: I don't know how I let myself get this big.

Me: You ate. A LOT. The amount you ate in a single sitting is enough to feed a house full of relatives in an African village.

Customer: How dare you!

Me: Yes. I did. I dared myself to take control of my life, and I did. I lost one hundred fifty pounds and so can you. Do you want to hear more about our program?

Customer: I don't know . . . is it expensive?

Me: It's five hundred dollars for the year plus the cost of food.

Customer: WHAT?! That's insane! I can't afford that!

Me: Let me ask you something. If your car broke down today, what would you do?

Customer: Fix it?

Me: Yes. Of course you would. What if it was going to cost you five thousand dollars and if you didn't fix it your car would blow up?

Customer: I'd pay it.

Me: Well, this is your life, which is way more valuable than a car. And you're willing to spend five grand on a hunk of metal but not five hundred on your LIFE? Now, does that make sense to you?

Customer: Wow. I never thought of it that way.

Me: That's why I'm here. Welcome to the family.

CHA-CHING.

I hate to say it, but I was the shit. And I wasn't lying when I gave my sales pitch. I believed every word I was saying. I really thought this job was what I was born to do . . . until it all ended.

I was early to work on that fateful day, strolling in at seven a.m. wearing the most unflattering outfit Macy's had to offer. I had been promoted the week before, so I had to up my game. Target wasn't gonna cut it anymore. I needed REAL silk; enough of that faux shit. My hair was bone straight and my pimply face clean shaven. I was ready to start the day. When I walked in I greeted everyone like they were my family, because after three years of working there, they were. I looked at my before-and-after picture, which was hanging on the wall in the lobby, and I gave it a good-luck fist bump. I walked back to my office and opened the door and saw a stranger sitting in my chair. She was fat, so I thought she was a new client.

> Me: Oh, I'm sorry. The waiting area is in the lobby. I'll be right out and I'll bring you back to weigh you. I'm excited to start this journey with you.

My hand reached out for a friendly shake. It was not received.

> Woman: I'm not a client, I'm from the corporate offices, Shane.
> Me: Really?

I looked her up and down. Not really the vision of health someone who works at a weight-loss corporate office should be, but who was I to judge?

Me: Ok. So . . . can I help you?

Woman: I'd like you to pack up all your stuff and be off the premises in five minutes.

Me: Um . . . what?

Woman: Time is ticking.

Stopwatch activated.

Me: What are you talking about? Is this a prank? Is this some kind of fat *Punk'd*? Is some fat Ashton Kutcher gonna pop out of the freezer room and yell GOTCHA?

Woman: I'm not Ashton Kutcher, Shane. Please pack your things.

Me: What did I do? Is it because of what I did in the bathroom yesterday during my lunch break? I didn't know there were cameras in there.

Woman: What?

Me: Huh? Nothing. Never mind.

I masturbated at work. A lot.

Me: So what did I do?

She told me. And I was pissed. Apparently I was fired because I had made a vlog at work. Now, this was back before EV-ERYONE vlogged so I guess the weight-loss center was freaked out that one of their employees was making strange internet videos at work. When in reality my vlogging was only promoting their company more. But it was 2009, so I can't hate them for not being "hip to the times." But what I am mad about is the way they handled the situation. Not only did they fire me, they fired all the other employees who were in my vlogs, and that included my mother and brother, who had started working for the company after I did. As I walked out of my office carrying all my belongings, I stopped and stood before my before-and-after poster.

Me: I'm taking this. And when I get famous I'm going to tell everyone that I lost my weight using your archrival, Nutrisystem!

Woman: Good luck with that.

Even though this was one of the worst days of my life, it was a blessing in disguise. It forced me to focus on my YouTube channel, which eventually was successful enough that I could buy my mom a house and even spend more than $20 for an outfit at Target. So in closing, I'd like to say thank you to the weight-loss center for firing me. Just like when I needed to quit my job as paperboy for my grandma to "explore my options," I needed to leave the world of weight loss to see what else was out there. And what I found was so much better. So for that I'm thankful.

Also, if you would like to lose weight and get in the best shape of your life, be sure to call 1-800-NUTRISYSTEM.

ASTRAL PROJECTION

ABOUT THE ARTIST

Christopher Daod became interested in art as a
student during his early years in primary school. He continues to practice his skill during his high school years. He
resides in Sydney, Australia, with his family. Follow him
on Instagram at @Chrissy_Daod.

've always been different. Not just in a "Wow, that kid is different, did his mom try and shove him down the toilet at prom?" kind of way. But in a spiritual way. I was never an avid churchgoer and I don't know the Bible cover to cover, but I've always had a strong connection with God and the spiritual world. When I was a kid I would just lie on my bed and talk to God for hours. On second thought, maybe I'm schizophrenic? Honestly, that would explain a lot.

Anyways, on the night I found out my parents were getting divorced I lay in bed and cried for hours. I was nine, and the thought of my entire world changing was overwhelming and too much to handle. I had already eaten all the Nutter Butters in the house, so I resorted to sobbing into my *Lion King* pillowcase. I felt a hand on my back and a soft, calm voice telling me, "It's gonna be ok." I turned over thinking I would see my mom sitting on my bed next to me but there was nobody there. I know I should have been freaked out but for some reason I was ok with the fact that some kind of spirit had just touched and spoken to me. Thinking back, that was creepy as shit and I can't believe I didn't piss my bed.

A year after that I started having really intense dreams. I was super close to my paternal grandmother, who had just died. Everyone always said when I grew up I would look just like her, which was disheartening, considering she was a morbidly obese woman who lived in a chair. She literally never got up from her chair during the last fifteen years of her life. She had her fridge within arms-grabbin' distance, and I'm pretty sure she peed into a Big Gulp cup. So my future was looking really bright.

The night after she died I had a dream that I floated out of my body and flew up into the sky. I could actually see myself lying in bed, and I could see my entire neighborhood as I floated away. When I got higher than the clouds I heard the voice of my grandmother. I turned to look at her and what I saw was a young woman in her twenties floating next to me with the biggest blue eyes I had ever seen. She had long, flowing hair and she was wearing a pink baby-doll dress. We had a long conversation about life, death, and even how she didn't want me to end up like her. She told me to stay strong and not let anybody get me down. She told me to quit emotionally eating and learn how to deal with pain by being creative and expressing myself. She said I was destined for greatness and she would be watching me every step of the way.

When I woke up the next day I ran to my mom's room and told her about the dream. I told her what Grandma looked like and how it was like a younger version of herself. My mom started crying and ran to the closet to get something. She grabbed an old photo album and flipped to a picture of my grandmother when she was in her twenties. She looked exactly like I'd dreamed she did. The big eyes, the long hair, and even the same pink baby-doll dress. My mom said that she believed when we die and go to heaven our body goes back to when we were the happiest. My grandma chose to go back to her youth, when she wasn't stuck to a chair. From that morning on I knew that I had some kind of strange connection to the spiritual world. Either that or eating two hundred Nutter Butters before going to sleep caused some seriously fucked-up hallucinations.

When I was thirteen I started having different kinds of dreams. They weren't conversations with dead people but instead dreams in which I would float around my neighborhood and spy on people. I know. That's creepier than talking to dead people, but trust me, if you were thirteen and could snoop on your neighbors, you would.

The first experience I had with this was one day after school when I decided to take a nap after watching about three hours of *Saved by the Bell* reruns. My family and I had just moved into a new apartment building that weekend and hadn't met any of our neighbors. I laid my head back and drifted off pretty quickly. Then I opened my eyes and started noticing that the ceiling was getting closer and closer to my face. I turned around and saw that I was floating out of my body. I hadn't done this in years, and I started panicking. I tried everything I could to get back into my body and wake up but nothing was working. It was honestly the scariest feeling I'd ever had. Well, that and the feeling I got when my school nurse made me take off my shirt in front of the whole class to give me a scoliosis test. That was traumatizing. One kid asked why my nipples looked sad. I don't quite know what he meant, but I also kinda know exactly what he meant.

As I floated farther away from my body I decided to just go with it and see where it was gonna take me. I went right through the front door like the Kool-Aid man. Except the door didn't blow up into a billion pieces. I just kinda dissolved through it. I floated through my new apartment building and saw some new faces. A blond lady walking her golden retriever, a young Asian kid riding a scooter, and a gardener obviously looking into a woman's window while she was changing clothes. My first thought was, "What a perv!" My second thought was, "I can probably float through that window!" But I held back and decided to go back to my body. I woke up in a huge sweat and let out a loud gasp. I instantly decided to pretend the dream was one of those that only *felt* super realistic. I totally disregarded the possibility that I could have actually floated outside my body.

RING RING. I jumped up and screamed like a big-tittied blonde in a horror movie. Why do phones always ring when I'm already on the edge of freaking the fuck out? I answered it and it was my mom asking me to come to the car to help her with some boxes. As I walked out the door I saw three things that would change my life forever: a blond lady walking her golden retriever, a young Asian kid riding a scooter, and a gardener looking into a woman's window while she was changing clothes. This was not a coincidence. This was something bigger.

Astral projection (or astral travel) is an interpretation of out-of-body experience (OBE) that assumes the exis-

tence of an astral body separate from the physical body
and capable of traveling outside it.

—Wikipedia

Now, I know this is hard to take in, and I'm sure a lot of you have started mentally checking out, but trust me, it's not bullshit. If I were bullshitting you, I would write a story about how hard it was being a kid in high school with a fifteen-inch penis that kept getting stepped on in the hallway. I'm sure that would make for a more interesting book.

If the term "astral projection" sounds familiar to you it's probably because you saw that 2010 horror film *Insidious*, about the kid who could float outside his body while dreaming. When I saw that movie I freaked out. I thought I was the only person who had ever experienced such a thing. And it didn't help that the kid in the movie floated down to hell and was enslaved by a pedophile demon that looked like Michael Jackson covered in menstrual blood. I'm surprised I ever slept again.

After watching the movie I went back home and started researching and learned that astral projection was incredibly common. Even some celebrities could do it, like Gary Busey and Shaq! Ok, I'm aware those aren't the best examples of people to trust, but hey, it's something.

That night I lay in bed and tried my hardest to float outside of my body. I thought maybe I could go and hang out with other floaters and talk about how cool we were because we could watch other people sleep. Who knows, maybe I could even become friends with Gary Busey and Shaq! Unfortunately nothing happened. A week later I went to sleep not expecting anything and of course that's when it happened. I had the most intense astral projection of my life. I was taking a nap in my garage, which, believe me, is not as weird and depressing as it sounds. My garage had been converted into an office and had a sick-ass couch that was so comfortable I could imagine becoming my fat, dead grandmother and living on it. As I drifted off to sleep my eyes began to open. But this time I couldn't float out of my body. Something was holding me back. I looked around the room and saw a black figure standing by the door. It didn't have a face and didn't have much of a shape. It was more like the essence of a person. I could hear it breathing and it started getting closer and closer to me. I tried everything I could to wake up but nothing was working. My heart was pounding and my stomach was churning like I was going to throw up. The figure got closer and closer but I still couldn't see its face. Then it put its hand, which looked more like a claw, on my chest and started pushing down. It felt like this presence was trying to get inside my body. Finally I woke up and jumped off my couch. I ran out of my garage and into the house. I knew what just happened wasn't good and was too real to be a nightmare.

I decided to do more research and what I found was truly frightening. Many people who astral-project have run into situations where they encountered an angry spirit that wanted to harm them. Some even said that the spirit tried to jump into their body while they were away from it. Their advice was to "will yourself back into your body when you start to feel threatened." Now, this all sounded like the scariest shit in the world and I never wanted to sleep again, but I knew that eventually the Red Bulls would wear off and I would have to face my demons . . . literally.

A few nights later, as I fell asleep in my bedroom, I decided that if any dark figures tried to mess with me I would just will myself back into my body and everything would be ok. What's the worst that could happen? I get possessed by some crazy demon, murder my entire family, and upload my confession on to my YouTube channel? As if!

So I fell asleep and once again opened my eyes. I was floating. I was out of my body and floating in my room. I had left the TV on and there was a rerun of *Diners, Drive-Ins and Dives* playing. If that spirit was to come back, hopefully the image of Guy Fieri choking down a ten-inch hoagie would scare him away. Just then I felt something was off. I was beginning to float out of my room but I looked back and saw the dark figure standing next to my body. I started panicking and felt my heart racing. I tried to close my eyes and will myself back into my body but it wasn't working. The figure looked up at me. This time it had a face. It wasn't human. It was almost animalistic. I decided to get up as much courage as I could and I floated toward the figure as fast as I could. I ran my spirit body into him and tackled him to the ground. It turned into a long, violent battle between me and this dark, cold mass. Then suddenly, I woke up. I was sweatier than I had ever been in my entire life. Even sweatier than when I found out zero-calorie butter spray is actually a thousand calories per bottle. Those fucking liars.

This had gotten out of hand. I didn't want to ever astral-project again. I'm not as strong as Gary Busey or Shaq. After reading up on people who have been in similar situations, I learned that to avoid astral projecting all you have to do is tell yourself, as you're falling asleep, that you aren't going to let it happen. So I started doing that. Slowly but surely I stopped and went back to having dreams about my entire family murdering me and eating my limbs for their survival. You know, normal dreams.

If you have ever astral-projected, don't be afraid to explore and float around, but remember, if it starts to get out of hand, don't continue it. I think Gary Busey and Shaq might still be out there floating around while some mentally challenged demons have taken over their bodies. Maybe Britney Spears is a projector? Wow. Now everything makes sense.

JUST A PRETTY FACE

ABOUT THE ARTIST

Anna Sofia Ellermann *is a twenty-one-year-old self-taught artist with a particular interest in photography and digital art. Born in Copenhagen, she now lives on the beautiful island of Bornholm in Denmark. Anna believes in a colorful life with respect for animals and all people. Follow her at @Heroine_red on Instagram and visit her website, www.Heroinered.com.*

As a young boy going through puberty there are a lot of things you hope people notice about you. Your newly grown leg hair, your barely there mustache, and most of all your deepening man voice. The last thing I would do every night before I fell asleep was pray to God that when I woke up I would have at least one of those three things. Ok, that's a lie. The last thing I did every night before going to sleep was violently hump my bed. I also used to pray that I would one day experience an orgasm. When you are a kid you don't really have a "release." You just have an urge to hump every object in your house. Sometimes even food. Am I going too far?

Let me get back on track and also away from discussing boy penis. I'm guessing there are legal ramifications for talking about that in a book. Anyways, every morning I would wake up the same. No leg hair, no mustache, and definitely not a deep voice. But the worst trait that I had was something no boy wants. I had a pretty face.

Now, I don't want this to sound cocky. I really did have a beautiful face. It was plump and round in all the right places. My cheekbones were high and sat perfectly under my Coke-bottle glasses, creating a cute little crease when I smiled. My lips were soft and shiny. My eyelashes were literally three inches long and made audible flapping sounds when I blinked. Like a fairy flying through the clouds. I'm still shocked and slightly offended that I was never molested. Even though my face was pretty I didn't have a haircut to match. It looked like I had gone into a Supercuts and asked: "Who here is suicidal and wants to leave the world with one last FUCK-YOU?" It was as if someone had put head shots of all the lesbians in Hollywood into a computer system and had all their hairstyles morphed into one Super-Mega-Lesbian haircut. If it was physically possible for Rosie O'Donnell and Ellen DeGeneres to breed they would have popped me out.

Because I looked so much like a woman I tried really hard to dress like a man. I would wear big flannel shirts, baseball hats, and cargo shorts with A LOT of pockets. But it only made it worse. I didn't look like a man, I just looked like a really butch lesbian. I looked like the giver in the relationship, if you know what I mean. I wore the pants and brought home the bacon. At our lesbian wedding, I put the ring on her finger and led our first dance. Which, side note, I went to a wedding recently and the first dance was to Elton John's "The Last Song." The whole time all I could think was, "Isn't this song about AIDS?" Bold choice.

But it wasn't just my looks that made me a little woman, it was my voice. I had the voice of a 1940s Hollywood darling. Every time I opened my mouth my grandmother would tell me how much I reminded her of Judy Garland. When a telemarketer would call they would start with "How are you today, ma'am?" This made it very easy for me to hang up on them guilt-free, so for that I'm grateful. But what was worse than my voice and my womanly exterior was the fact that my best friend was my mother. So not only did I look and sound like a chick, but ALL my interests were of the female persuasion. "JO-ANN CRAFT STORE ON A SATURDAY?! YOU DON'T GOTTA ASK ME TWICE!"

My mom and I would drive around the city for hours blaring Paula Abdul and talk about how much my father didn't understand us. We would get fro yo with extra toppings because it was our "cheat day" and because "we deserved it." I even remember going to a lingerie shop to help her find something for her anniversary. She wanted something sassy yet functional and nothing that screamed, "I'm willing to try anal." That last part I just assumed because she never wanted anything with "butt fringe."

Sometimes we would refer to ourselves as Thelma and Louise. Looking back I realize how unhealthy and disturbing that is, but back then it was great. I loved spending hours watching chick flicks and braiding my mom's hair. And don't get me started on how good I was at balling melon. I was the melon-balling QUEEN. If my mom had died I think I would have been able to take her place pretty easily. I mean, having sex with my father would have been weird, but I'm sure I could have adjusted. Everything was great until one day my whole mama's-boy world came crashing down.

It was a really hot day, and my boy tits were dripping. I was lying on the couch with a Weight Watchers ice-cream bar, enjoying everything Montel Williams had to offer. Usually it was just rants about MS, but sometimes he'd have a psychic come on and tell people their lost kids were dead, and that was pretty interesting. My mom walked into the kitchen tying her huge red hair into a bun and opened the refrigerator to get a cold breeze. She put her ass against the vegetable drawer and moaned like a dog getting scratched in all the right places. We couldn't afford air-conditioning so it was up to us to find our own source of cold air. We had to get really creative. One time I put a pair of my underwear in the freezer and wore them the next day. I still blame that incident for why my flaccid penis is so shriveled to this day.

"Let's get out of here," my mom said as she wrung the sweat out of her tumbleweed-like hair.

"To the movies? We kind of already saw *Titanic* eight times. I don't think I can handle that kind of emotional distress again." I had already cried all day because I found out Weight Watchers had changed their point system and it no longer included "free foods." Nazi assholes.

"No, let's go to the beach!" mom squealed. My body froze. The beach was not a happy place for me. There were way too many variables that made it uncomfortable. Everyone was half-naked. Homeless couples kissed each other in the shade. There was bird shit EVERYWHERE. And worst of all my skin would burn instantly. It was like putting a wrapped Ding Dong in the microwave. Wait. Is that reference too fat for the general public? Ok, Ding Dongs have a foil wrapper that makes them flammable when put in microwaves. Sorry for expecting you to know that.

We packed up our stuff and got in the car. Even though I hated the beach, at least I knew there would be a breeze, and that was better than melting in my shitty apartment. As we got close we started looking at all the cool beach houses and talking about how awesome it would be to live in one someday. We were lesbians planning out our lives together. One day we would have a house on the sand, a big golden retriever, and a "themed room." You know, like a reading room that looked like a jungle, or a scrapbooking room that had lots of pictures of babies in weird costumes everywhere. Something classy and tasteful.

We pulled up to the parking lot and found a spot right away. We were always really lucky when it came to that stuff. My mom would say, "God is with us!" and I would always think, "Shouldn't God be helping all the big-stomached children in Africa instead of helping us get parking spots?" But hey, a spot's a spot. We got our stuff out of the trunk and lugged it to a nice area on the sand. Right in between a trash can with CUM DUMPSTER spray-painted on it and a family of twenty celebrating somebody's "*cumpleaños*." We lay down on our shared towel and I started rubbing her down with suntan lotion. Not in a creepy way, she just couldn't reach her back. Also, I have a really soothing touch. It's one of my many gifts. That and I can tell someone they have a booger hanging out of their nose just by looking at them a certain way.

We laughed the afternoon away and ate massive amounts of Otter Pops. It was the perfect summer day. And then it was ruined by one dumb visor-wearing bitch with a chest sunburn and spider veins. She walked by with her husband and their ugly dog and said, "I don't have a problem with lesbians, but I just don't want to look at them." My heart sank. I don't know what hurt more, the fact that she was obviously a homophobe or the fact that she thought I was a woman. Not a little girl. A FULL-BLOWN WOMAN. I was only twelve! Sure, I had a pretty face and some perky breasts, but wasn't it obvious that I was a CHILD?

My mom pretended she didn't hear it and changed the subject. "Hey! You know Oreo is coming out with a new flavor this month. I think it's Creamsicle!"

NO, MOM! You can't make me forget what just happened! Not even if Oreo is coming out with something that sounds REVOLUTIONARY AND FUCKING DELICIOUS. I will not just sit here and ignore what that bitch just said! "Mom . . . Do people really think I'm a girl?"

My mom's silence told me everything I needed to know.

The next year of my life was hell. I was called ma'am everywhere I went. I wouldn't even set foot in a Sizzler because I was constantly mistaken for a waitress. I tried everything I could to be more manly. I shaved my hairless face, thinking maybe that would speed up the five o'clock shadow process. Instead that just gave me lots of face cuts and a mental scar after I found out it was my mom's "everything" razor. I tried stuffing my crotch with socks, but that just looked like I had a fat vagina. I asked my older brother for advice and he said: "Just wait it out. One day you'll wake up and look in the mirror and see a man. I promise."

So I waited. Every morning for the next year I would run to the mirror to see if anything had changed. Besides the fact that I was getting taller and fatter, I didn't notice much difference. But then one night shortly after my thirteenth birthday I took a trip to PetSmart with my mom. As we were checking out, the man at the register handed me our bag and said words I had never heard before. Words I had waited for my whole life. Words that seem stupid to the average person but to me meant everything. He said, "Have a nice night, sir."

SIR. He called me SIR! I was overwhelmed with emotion. I started crying and grabbed my mother for a hug. He had NO idea what was going on, and I'm sure he thought I had some kind of disorder, but I didn't care. This was MY MOMENT, and I was TAKING IT! And that night when my mom and I went out for fro yo it wasn't just because it was our "cheat day." I really did feel like I "deserved it." From that day forward I was a man. Not just on the inside but on the outside as well. Thank you, random PetSmart cashier. You changed my life.

MY LEG TWIN

ABOUT THE ARTIST

Jerad Garcia is thirteen years old and has never taken an art class. His love for drawing began when he was little and became stronger during middle school. Follow him on Twitter at @nyanjerbear.

You know how you walk around the city and stare at everyone's bodies and compare theirs to your own? No? Just me? Well, it's a habit I picked up when I was around eleven years old and already fixated on my weight. It probably didn't help that I went to my first Weight Watchers meeting when I was ten, but that's beside the point. Walking around school, I would stare at every guy's body and wonder what he looked like naked. It wasn't a sexual thing, it was more of an "I wonder if they have that weird fold of fat above their privates too" type of thing.

I always felt like I had a bizarre body that was a scientific anomaly. I had the face and arms of a thin person but the stomach and legs of someone who bleeds marshmallow fluff and Nutella. It was kind of like I was an actor sitting in my trailer halfway out of my fat suit. They'd taken off the face prosthetics but I still had the bodysuit on.

My brother was the total opposite. He had the shape and coloring of a carrot. I was never jealous of his red hair, but I would have made a deal with Satan to get a body like his. I couldn't imagine what it would feel like to pick up a pair of pants at the store and not have to make adjustments to the waistline with a steak knife and scissors when I got home. And by the way, a 4X shirt isn't much different from a 3X shirt, so don't waste your money on the extra X. It's a scam, and it's sad that I know that.

The fixation with my weird body didn't go away when I lost weight. In fact, it got worse. I still to this day walk around checking out other dudes' bodies and comparing them to my own. On my first date with a girl she noticed that I was checking out guys in the restaurant and started getting suspicious. That mixed with my haircut, four coatings of high-gloss ChapStick, and skinny jeans with decorative fading didn't help my case. I tried to explain to her that I wasn't checking out their packages, I was merely checking out the rest of them and doing their measurements in my head. This didn't go over well and dinner ended early. But it gave me an excuse to go home and watch an extra hour of *My 600-lb Life* on my DVR, so it all worked out.

One day a few years back I was lying in bed contemplating whether or not I should brush my teeth but instead watched twelve hours of children's television. I have a sick obsession with children's television. I don't know if it's because I enjoy terrible jokes and loud fart sound effects or . . . actually that's exactly what it is. That explains my humor perfectly. Mystery solved.

Anyways, I was about eight hours into the season of some terrible Disney show when I noticed one of the guest stars had MY LEGS. They were chubby, wide at the hips, and shaped like a pork chop. I paused my TV and stared at it for a good ten minutes. I had never seen a guy with my legs before. I'd seen plenty of five-months-pregnant women with my legs but never a man. He had a soft middle like me and his body was SO disproportionate that it made me feel like I had a long-lost twin. I always wondered if that birthmark on my ass was from a twin-separation surgery! Mom always said it was "a kiss from an angel." THAT LYING CUNT.

I knew I had a twin and it was my mission to find him. So I did what any sane twenty-three-year-old man would do. I looked him up on IMDb, then found his Twitter, then tweeted him till he followed me so I could direct-message him to set up a time to meet up. Yup. Totally sane.

Two days later I woke up to a new Twitter notification on my phone. HE'D FOLLOWED ME BACK. Score! I tried to think of some small talk that would make it seem like I'd just stumbled across his Twitter and decided to follow him. I didn't want to tell him the truth because something told me "YOU'RE MY FAT-LEG TWIN!" wouldn't go over well. After a few small-talk conversations he asked me if I wanted to hang out. My heart stopped. I felt like a twelve-year-old girl getting asked out by my biggest crush. Except I wasn't sexually interested in him; I was just interested in his pork chop thighs. So I told him that I was pretty busy but I could try and fit it in. I liked playing hard to get with my leg twin. He gave me a time and location and it was on and crackin'. Same time next day, I was going to see my other legs in person! I couldn't wait! I prayed to God that it would be a thousand degrees so he would show up in shorts. I didn't know what I would do if his legs were chubby AND hairy like mine. I thought I would actually have a full-on mental breakdown. The feeling of joy would overtake my body and make my fat legs explode.

The next day I pulled up to the coffee shop where we were going to meet and waited in the car. I got there a little early because I wanted to see him walk in. I wanted to see those legs in motion. I got a text from him saying that he was running a few minutes late. I told him not to worry about it and that I was running late too. Lies. I had been there for almost thirty minutes in anticipation of this epic moment. I started to get nervous. The reality of what was happening hit me. What if he walked up to the coffee shop and his legs were skinny? Would I just take off? It started feeling like a PlentyOfFish date. I was already planning my escape. And as I was planning I looked up out the window and I saw them. They were standing right in front of the coffee shop. Thick, sausaged into tight jeans, and beautiful. They looked even fatter in person, just like mine! I started sweating. This was it, the big moment; I was ready. I hopped out of my car and walked up to him. I was hoping that maybe he would look at my legs and notice that we were leg twins. I even tried to mimic his walk so that he would get some kind of leg déjà vu. Unfortunately he wasn't as creepy and body obsessed as me, so he didn't look below my face.

Leg Twin: Hey, Shane!

Me: Hey!

Leg Twin: This is so weird! I've been watching you online for a while now!

Me: I've been watching you too!

Leg Twin: Really? On what?

Me: Your Disney show!

Leg Twin: Aren't you twenty-three?

Me: Who wants coffee?!

I walked him into the café and found us a table. As we walked over I stared at him from behind. He didn't just have my legs, he had my ENTIRE BODY! This was a miracle! We sat down and made small talk. I don't remember anything we talked about because I was staring at his chest the entire time. I could see his lopsided nipples poking through his exercise shirt and all I could think was, "I wonder if they have black spots around the areolas too?!" I started undressing him in my head and I'm gonna be honest, it got super creepy. Once again, this wasn't a homoerotic experience, it was more of an unwrapping-gifts-on-Christmas-Eve experience. I just wanted to rip off all his clothes and rub my twin body against his and take a bunch of selfies!

A waitress walked over and asked for our order. I was hoping to God that he would order the same thing as me just to make this man date even more magical. But what happened was shocking and a sign of things to come.

Waitress: What would you boys like today?

Me: I'll take a side of fries and extra ranch, please! And a
      Diet Coke with a cherry in it!

Waitress: How old are you? Ten?

Leg Twin: And he watches the Disney Channel!

Waitress: [laughs] He must be the slow brother!

She thought we were BROTHERS. PERFECT!

Waitress: And what would you like, baby?
Leg Twin: Can I just get a grilled chicken breast, no oil, no
    butter, no sauce?
Waitress: Of course. Diet Coke too?
Leg Twin: GOD NO. That stuff will kill you.

Oh no. This had just taken a turn. We were not brothers.
We weren't even in the same forest of family trees. We probably weren't even going to be friends. The waitress walked away
and I just stared at him in silence for a few moments. I didn't
know what to say. If he ate that healthy how in God's name did
he have my body? He must have just started some new diet to
shed the puffiness.

Me: So. On a diet?
Leg Twin: No way. I don't consider it a diet. More of a life-
    style.

WHO THE FUCK IS THIS? THIS IS NOT MY TWIN.

Me: Oh . . . so you have always eaten like that?
Leg Twin: Oh ya, your body is a temple, ya know? Gotta
    keep it clean!
Me: Right . . . temple . . .

Leg Twin: You used to be fat, right?

Me: Ya. How did you know that?

Leg Twin: You made a video about it. And you are always retweeting pictures of food porn. It's actually sad sometimes. You retweeted a picture of raw cookie dough last night at three a.m.

Me: Ya, it was a tough day.

Leg Twin: You should come work out with me some time!

WORK . . . OUT . . . ? Ok, there was NO way with that soft puffy body this dude worked out. Unless he worked out and then did a keg stand for twelve hours immediately after.

Me: Ya. Maybe. You go often?

Leg Twin: Oh ya, every day. There's nothing I love more than sweating so much that I can wring my shirt out and fill an empty Gatorade bottle with it!

I had to agree with him on that. Except replace "sweat" with "pee" and replace "Gatorade bottle" with "Diet Coke bottle." I don't need that wide a mouth.

Leg Twin: Oh God. You ever get an itch on your back that you just can't reach?

And this was the moment when all my dreams came crashing down. As he reached his arm to scratch his lower back, his shirt lifted up and revealed something that I never saw coming.

A MOTHERFUCKING SIX-PACK. This guy wasn't soft! This guy was hard! Harder than a priest during a baptism! Harder than the dad from *7th Heaven* during the "Ruthie rides a horse" episode! How does a body so fit look so soft in clothing? Why does my body look like shit in clothing AND naked? I had so many questions flying through my head that I started seeing stars.

Leg Twin: I'm gonna go to the bathroom. Be right back!

As he got up to leave I stared at his legs and realized that he didn't have chubby legs, he had THICK legs! There's a HUGE difference! His thighs were thick because they were so RIPPED! He could have crushed a watermelon with those pork chop thighs!

I instantly started feeling sick to my stomach. I had built this man up in my head to be my clone and instead he was just a better version of me. A better version of me with more credits on his IMDb page.

Now, I want to be clear: I'm not a fat guy and I don't think I am, but I definitely am a guy who should lift more weights and not have ranch with every meal. I lost a bunch of weight, but I've never been able to get toned. I just don't have the willpower to hit up the gym every day for two hours, and the idea of cutting candy out of my diet seems impossible. So because of that I just have to live with the fact that I'll never be able to take my shirt off in public, and I'm OK with that.

I started contemplating my escape plan. Should I just leave and pretend like I had been taken away by the rapture?

Should I leave a note telling him that my family died and I had to go identify the bodies? I was desperate for a way out of this disaster.

He walked back to the table and sat down with a satisfied look on his face. I'm sure he had just taken a huge, healthy bowel movement and here I was with IBS and a stomach full of ranch dressing that was sure to come out my ass like I got bukakked at a gang bang. I ended the conversation and told him I had a lot of work to do at home, and I wasn't lying. I had about four hours of standing in front of the mirror looking at my body in and out of clothes to look forward to. As we left we decided that sometime soon we were going to hang out again, but he didn't know the truth. I had already gotten what I wanted out of this relationship. I was ready to move on. I saw what he was working with and decided it wasn't for me. The last thing I needed was another friend who was comfortable taking their shirt off at the beach. So we went our separate ways and never spoke again.

This entire situation showed me that I shouldn't be looking for a body twin. I shouldn't even be looking at myself that much, because nobody really cares about how I look except for me. I have this idea that when I walk around in public everyone is judging me or comparing my body to theirs, when in reality the only people who are doing that are me and maybe a few other mentally unstable people. All that Disney star wanted to do was hang out and possibly start a friendship, but instead I shut him out of my life because I didn't want to be reminded of how fat I felt around him. Luckily in the last few years I have gotten over the constant need to check out dudes' physiques, and hopefully one day me and Disney dude will cross paths again and get some oil-free, butter-free, fat-free chicken together. Until then, I will continue to lie on my bed retweeting food porn and watching television shows I'm criminally too old for.

SHOCKTUBER

ABOUT THE ARTIST

Samantha Gleason *is a young artist from the suburbs of Philadelphia. She started drawing during her freshman year of high school. Her Instagram page, where she posts all her work, has more than 100,000 followers. The constant support has kept her motivated to draw. Go to samonstage.com to find out more.*

One a.m. The sound of thousands of robotic birds chirping repeatedly filled my room. This could only mean one of two things. Either I was finally having that "nervous breakdown" my mother told me was hereditary, or my Twitter was blowing the fuck up. I didn't have the urge to shave my head and jump out my bedroom window, so it must have been the latter.

When my Twitter blows up my first thought is, "OH MY GOD LINDSAY LOHAN DIED." Every morning when I wake up I wonder if the number-one trending topic in the world is gonna be #RIPLINDSAY right above #SHEWASSOGOODIN MEANGIRLSWHATHAPPENED. I mean, not to sound morbid, but it's just a matter of time, right? I think we are all just waiting for it. We want her to make it through, but let's keep it real: ticktock.

Anyways, my Twitter wasn't blowing up because of a former child star's death or even because of another hurricane with a waitress's name. It was blowing up because I was supposedly "a racist."

There are few words that actually offend me. Putting my life out on the internet for so long has made me numb to pretty much every criticism and insult. I got a comment on a video once that said, "I bet your grandmother is looking up from hell crying because you are such a stupid cock sucking faggot with aids," and my first thought was, "Shouldn't 'AIDS' be capitalized?" So not much bothers me. But when people say I'm racist it really gets under my skin. My superior, perfect, white skin.

So you are probably wondering what set Twitter off. What set Twitter ablaze wasn't even anything I had done but something that people ASSUMED I had. It was a sketch on You-Tube about Harriet Tubman making a sex tape and it went viral after CNN got ahold of it. Because some of the actors in the video are actors I have used in some of my work, people assumed I created it. Which was completely untrue and really frustrated me. I would NEVER do a video about Harriet Tub-man making a sex tape. Cameras weren't even around back then. I take creative liberties in my sketches, but I don't want them to be completely inaccurate!

As I scrolled through my timeline I saw thousands of "SHANE DAWSON IS RACIST" and "SHANE DAWSON HATES BLACK PEOPLE" tweets and each one was like a dagger in my heart. The angry mob started posting links to other videos I had done and pointing out every offensive joke I had ever made. They started creating a narrative that I was this secret KKK member who was out to brainwash the youth of Amer-ica with my sick racist comedy. Which is ridiculous. If I were trying to brainwash the youth of America I would brainwash them into buying more merch. My merch doesn't really sell that well. It's unfortunate because it's good shit.

But I digress. I tried to set the record straight and explain that I had nothing to do with the video, but that went unheard. The fire was too big and no amount of explanation could put it out. So I waited. It eventually blew over and I went back to waiting for Lindsay Lohan to die.

But this wasn't the first time I'd been labeled a racist. My videos have been controversial since I first started back in 2008. The "did he really just say that" and "whoa too far Shane!" comments have been flooding my YouTube channel since the beginning. But I never set out to be some kind of shocktuber (just made up that term; feel free to use it). Pushing the envelope is just something that I naturally do without even trying. It's second nature to me, like riding a bike or making an audible sad-sigh sound when I walk by a homeless person. I can't help it. My humor was created by my environment. Margaret Cho isn't considered a racist for making jokes about Asians and their stereotypes because it's what she grew up with. It's what she knew. And the same goes for me.

I grew up in Long Beach, California, where we are famous for raising Snoop Dogg and having lots of stabbings. All my jokes, all my characters, all my points of view as a comedian were created while living in that environment. I'm sure as I get older I will be influenced by new experiences, but for now I still grab from that period of my life.

My first time performing for an audience was in tenth grade. It was a sketch I wrote, and my drama teacher chose it to be performed in front of my entire tenth-grade class. It was about a white kid who wanted to fit in with his black friends, so he tried everything he could think of to impress them. It was a sketch full of stereotypes, and to an all-white audience it would probably have been received with crickets and uncomfortable silence. But to my diverse class it was received with uproarious laughter and a standing ovation. And to get tenth graders to stand for ANYTHING is a huge victory.

That day after the performance one of my teachers, who was white, asked me if I thought the skit was racist. I was shocked. How could satire be considered racist? I hadn't said anything demeaning, I hadn't used words that were hurtful, and I sure as hell hadn't said I was superior to anyone. Luckily I had a friend stick up for me and risk getting detention doing so. My friend happened to be black.

Friend: How was what he did racist?

Teacher: He was showcasing stereotypes. He was encouraging people to laugh at African-Americans and the way they act.

Friend: But some of us do act like that.

Teacher: Well, that doesn't make it right!

Friend: No, it makes it relatable. I KNOW people who act foolish and coonlike. And those people are ridiculous to me. Shane wasn't making fun of BLACK PEOPLE, he was making fun of a group of black people who act ridiculous.

Teacher: Well, I disagree.

Friend: Well, you're not black. You don't understand what it feels like for white people to walk on eggshells around us. Scared to say anything that could be misconstrued as racist. Making us feel like we should be treated with kid gloves because we can't take the fact that our skin is a different color and some people don't like us. I LIKE laughing at shit I relate to. And I like that a white person was doing it. It made me feel more a part of this society and less like an outcast.

Now, I know it sounds like I'm making that conversation up. It's too perfect and too well crafted to be an actual conversation between a high school student and his teacher. But it really happened. And it really changed the way I thought about comedy. There are things people are afraid to joke about, things people think are taboo, but I don't want to ever be afraid to go into that territory. Everybody just wants to relate and feel like a comedian "gets them." I think it's the reason I have such a diverse audience on YouTube. Because I truly relate to people who feel like they don't belong. I might be a white guy who hasn't been ignored by a taxi driver, but that doesn't mean I don't know what it's like to have people treat me like shit for being different. I don't ever make jokes that are hateful for no reason. If one of my characters says something completely over the line and offensive, the audience isn't meant to be laughing with them, they are meant to be laughing at them. Laughing at how stupid the character is for saying something so horrible, because there are people in this world who say horrible, stupid shit. And instead of just sitting back and taking it, I like to make fun of them.

Now, I can't control it if some racist person watches my

video and laughs for the wrong reason. That would be like not making horror movies because you don't want to give serial killers something to jerk off to. Every viewer has a different experience while watching something. All I can do is hope that my audience "gets it" and enjoys it.

One week later. One a.m. I hear the sound of thousands of robotic birds chirping repeatedly in my room. I rush to the computer. Has it finally happened? Is this it? I open up my browser and check the trending topics of the day. Nope, she's still alive. Just another hurricane with a waitress's name.

PROM

ABOUT THE ARTIST

Ashley D'Altilio *is an honor student at Pace University in New York City. Art has been a hobby of hers since she was only six years old, and she plans to continue with it. Originally from New Jersey, Ashley is a volunteer firefighter who loves traveling and learning foreign languages. She has been a Shane Dawson fan since 2008 and hopes to one day change lives like he has. Follow her on Twitter at @ashleysnotcool.*

A wise person once said: "Prom is only for whores and for the guys who want to fuck them." My grandma was a smart woman. Don't even get me started on her thoughts on *quinceañeras*. I'll give you a hint: they're horribly offensive and completely accurate. Anyways, there are so many people who will tell you that prom is a magical night full of romance and stomach butterflies, but they forget to tell you about the pain and embarrassment that come along with it. My prom experience was like watching a deadly car crash in slow motion. Heads were flying through the windshield, airbags were breaking people's skulls, and there was even a cute puppy smashed up against the hood getting sucked into the grille. It wasn't just the big night that was a disaster, it was the entire lead-up. So I'll take you through it slowly so you can get the whole sad, bloody picture. If you have any sharp objects or pill bottles nearby, hide them in a cupboard. This entire experience might throw you into a suicidal state.

One day during my thrilling senior year I was hanging out with my group of friends at lunch talking about all the exciting things going on in our lives. It was always a very short conversation. You know how every school has what's commonly known as "the crazy tree"? Well, if you don't know what I'm talking about, let me explain. During lunchtime all the cliques hung out in their designated sectors outside. Nobody hung out in the cafeteria because that's where the school food was, and being within ten feet of that would give you the stomach flu.

I don't know who decided on the sectors; I feel like it was a natural instinct thing. For example, I would NEVER have even dreamed of walking up to the benches by the school's side gate. That was an area filled with jocks who were getting pocket hand jobs from their cheerleader girlfriends. Just walking by, your nose would fill with the smell of splooge and hot Cheetos. The rest of the sectors were taken up by the nerds, the Asians, the black kids, the Mexicans, and the pregnant girls.

Finally, on the far side of the quad next to the girls' bathroom was a large tree that looked like it had been ripped out of some depressing Tim Burton movie. It created more shade than all the queens on *RuPaul's Drag Race* combined. If the tree could have spoken, it would have said, "Dear God, cut me the fuck down. I hate my life." It would probably also have asked that one fat girl to stop practicing her make-out skills on it. But that fat girl would never have stopped. That fat girl was me, and that tree marked my sector.

My group was made up of misfits, and not in the fun comic-book way, more in the rejected-scraps-of-meat-that-become-bologna way. I would say I was the leader of the group, but that implies that we did stuff that required leading. We more or less just stood around and shared a family-sized bag of Doritos. First there was Tara, who I told you about earlier. Although she wasn't usually around at lunchtime because she was in the parking lot "hanging out" with her guy friends. Then there was a four-foot-tall stoner named Pam who had an undiagnosed case of Tourette's syndrome. Her vocabulary was limited to cuss words that she would somehow combine to make full sentences.

Me: Hey, Pam. What's up?
Pam: Fuckin' bullshit bitch. Motherfuckers dumb-ass fuckin' with that bitch again. Shit.

She was a true linguist. Then there was Brandon, who was a loose cannon with slight serial-killer tendencies. One time he brought a Taser gun to school and gave Pam five bucks to let him try it on her. I don't remember exactly how it went down, but I do remember she almost died. Finally there was my lesbian friend and future prom date, Kelley. Did I mention she was a lesbian? Ya, we'll get to that later.

Kelley was a unique girl. Her wardrobe was a mix between Kenny from *South Park* and that guy who shot all his classmates in that one news story. There was lots of camo, lots of cargo pockets, and lots of stickers on her backpack that said "Aliens > People." She was a true freak, which is why we had so much in common. Kelley and I spent pretty much every weekend together. We would eat mass amounts of junk food, we would drive around while blaring Britney Spears and TELL NO ONE, and most important, we would make sketch comedy videos. Some of my first videos I ever posted on YouTube were ones we had made together. We had a great working relationship. I would hold the camera and force her to do whatever I wanted her to in front of it. In one video she had to give herself a fake abortion and then smear the blood on her face. Trust me, it's funnier than it sounds.

So it was the week before prom and everyone was planning out their epic romantic night of dancing and sex. Those of us under the crazy tree were more focused on who was going to get to pour the crumbs at the bottom of the Dorito bag down their throat that day.

Then the unthinkable happened. I was asked to prom.

Now, before you start imagining some amazing, beautiful moment when a girl walked up to me with a hand-painted sign that said PROM? and flower petals falling from the sky, let me share with you the bleak reality. Get ready for this. Once again, hide the sharp objects.

Kelley: Hey, Shane, can I talk to you over there for a second?

Me: By the trash can on fish stick day? This must be important.

Kelley: So . . . Do you want to go to prom with me?

Me: Um . . . what?

Kelley: I'm serious.

Me: You're a lesbian. Like a big lesbian. You constantly have new scabs on your forearms.

Kelley: What does that have to do with being a lesbian?

Me: I don't know. But it doesn't scream "I like dick."

Kelley: You wouldn't have to pay for it.

Me: Why? Is this a Make-A-Wish thing? Did the principal put you up to this? I keep telling him I'm not dying, I just have that dying-kid resting face.

Kelley: No. My dad is going to pay.

Me: Why? He doesn't even like paying for shampoo. I mean, your hair has more grease dripping from it than a deep fryer at the county fair.

Kelley: You really know how to make a girl feel pretty.

Me: Ok, what's going on? For reals.

Kelley: My dad wants me to go with a guy, so he said he would pay for you to go with me.

Me: Yikes. That's like the plot for some terrible nineties movie. Does it end with you realizing you're not gay and actually in love with me?

Kelley: I'm really glad we're next to a trash can right now. I feel chunks rising.

Me: So . . . If I say no, then what?

Kelley: Then I don't get to go to prom.

Me: Do you really want to go? A bunch of straight people fondling each other doesn't really sound like your thing.

Kelley: I know it's dumb, but I really want to go. The only time I've ever worn a dress was at my grandma's funeral a few years ago and I didn't even get to enjoy it. I had to change into something that would cover up my boobs while I helped carry the casket.

Me: Ya, funerals are tough.

Kelley: So what do you say? For me?

This was a hard decision. I didn't know what would hurt more, letting my friend down or going to the prom with a lesbian. It was like choosing between lice and crabs. One was contagious, the other would only affect me. I also didn't quite know how I felt about her dad pimping me out like I was some fat hooker. The sad part is what she said to sweeten the deal.

Kelley: My dad said he would pay for our Denny's meal.

The even sadder part was my reaction.

Me: I'M FUCKIN' IN!

So it was settled: Kelley was all mine for the night at the low cost of prom tickets, my tux, and my Denny's meal. The night of the prom arrived in a flash. Before I knew it, it was time for me to lie on the floor and have my mom help me zip up my tuxedo pants. As I put on my suit and looked in the mirror I couldn't help but notice how much I looked like a lesbian myself. Maybe this was meant to be. Maybe Kelley and I would be the hottest lesbian couple at the prom. Although we did have some pretty stiff competition. There were these two Cambodian girls who'd deejay at birthday parties on the weekends. They were pretty cool.

So I hopped in my never-been-washed car and headed over to my date's house. I picked up that wrist flower thing on the way there and then accidentally sat on it. To say it was destroyed would be an understatement. I did to that wrist flower thing what God did to the dinosaurs. EXTINCT.

As I pulled up to Kelley's house I started getting nervous. I'm not sure why, because it wasn't even a real date. But there was something about the suit, the romantic song playing on the radio, and the crushed corsage in between my ass cheeks that made me get stomach butterflies. Maybe this was what all those people were talking about. Maybe this night was going to be magical. Or maybe I was having bubble guts from all the sheet cake and refried beans I'd had the night before.

I got to the front door and before I could knock it swung open and I was hit with a storm of flashing lights. It was a photographer who her father had hired and he wasn't shy about getting all the shots he wanted. There were so many flashes I started to wonder if I was having a stroke. Which was totally possible, once again, considering the sheet cake and refried beans.

After the lights stopped flashing I looked up and saw Kelley standing in front of me looking like a completely different person. She wasn't the camouflaged, metal-tipped-hiking-boot-wearing girl I was used to. She was a beautiful princess with a dress perfectly fitted and a hairstyle ripped out of *Seventeen* magazine. No wonder she had to change her outfit at that funeral. She was probably giving the priest a chub. Well . . . probably not the priest; maybe the altar boys.

Me: Wow! You look great!

Kelley: I feel kind of stupid.

Me: Why?! You look amazing! You look like a child prostitute but happy about it!

Kelley: That's what I was going for.

Her dad walked out with a proud look on his face. He asked us to pose for a picture together and we took a few hundred. I'm sure I looked terrible in every one, but it didn't matter. She was pretty enough for the both of us. Her dad walked over to me and gave me the "take care of her" speech, which was incredibly uncomfortable but also kind of sweet.

I'm sure most people reading this are thinking he's an asshole for not letting his daughter go to prom with a girl but this was 2006. I know that doesn't feel like that long ago, but it really was. There weren't many openly gay kids at school and the only openly gay guy in Hollywood was Lance Bass, so there weren't many people to look up to. It's not like nowadays, where you throw a rock into a crowd and you hit ten gay dudes and five lesbians. Back in '06 there was only an LGB club at school, and now there's an LGBTGIA community. It's pretty amazing what eight years can do.

So our night was off to a good start and it was time to make it even better. We met up with some of our crazy tree friends at a restaurant, just like they do in all those teenager movies. I imagined all of us sitting around in our fancy outfits talking about the sexual adventures we were excited about having that night, but what I got was me and a few of our friends sharing a plate of Taterchos at a Denny's next to a free clinic.

If you don't know what Taterchos are, they were a limited option at Denny's in 2006. Instead of chips, they used tater tots for their nachos, and they were as brutal on your anus as you'd expect.

So as we sat around stuffing our faces with something only

homeless people should have been eating out of a trash can, one of my friends grabbed my leg with the strength of an ape. I'm not going to reveal my friend's name because what happened next should never happen to anyone ever. Especially at Denny's.

Nameless Friend: [whispering] Shane. I have a problem.
Me: What's wrong?
Nameless Friend: I got a visitor, if you know what I mean.
Me: Oh God, is your cousin Billy gonna stay with you again?
     He's the worst. You know every TV show theme song
     ever. WE GET IT.
Nameless Friend: No. I have a visitor. You-know-where.

As she pointed to her vagina it took about 5.5 seconds for it all to sink in. My eyes bulged out of my head and I made a loud gasp that was heard by the entire restaurant. What can I say, I'm smooth.

Kelley: What's going on?
Me: Huh? Oh, nothing. Tot down the wrong pipe.
Kelley: You breathed in a tater tot?
Me: Are you really surprised?
Kelley: I guess not.

Everyone went back to their tots and I turned to my nameless friend. Did I mention she was wearing a WHITE DRESS? The blood on her dress was as obvious as a skid mark on a pair of tighty whities, and trust me, I know my skid-marked tighty whities.

Me: What are you going to do?

Nameless Friend: I don't know! Can you cover for me?

Me: Like . . . spill ketchup all over you so they don't see the blood?

Nameless Friend: How did you come up with that plan so fast?

Me: When I was a kid I used to pee my pants, so my brother would dump soda on my lap to hide it.

Nameless Friend: Wow. That's so sweet and incredibly sad.

Me: So do you want me to do it?

Nameless Friend: I don't know! Isn't that worse? Smelling like ketchup at prom and having a huge stain on my dress? Maybe I can just pretend the blood is ketchup.

Me: Ketchup isn't that dark. Unless it's organic, and trust me, people know Denny's doesn't do organic.

Nameless Friend: Ok, fine. Do it.

So I took a deep breath and then casually squirted a huge pile of ketchup into her lap. I played it off like my hand had slipped, and everyone bought it.

Kelley: Shane! Oh my God! What the fuck?!

Me: Crap! I'm so sorry! I was so excited about the tots that I lost control of my motor skills!

Nameless Friend: It's ok! I'll just go to the bathroom and try to clean it off.

Kelley: Here, I'll go with you and help.

Everyone else at the table stared at me in confusion. I'm guessing they knew something was up, but then our milkshakes came to the table so they were quickly distracted.

After that bloody ordeal it was time to head to the prom. We got to the hotel where the party was happening and it was way fancier than I had expected. There were hanging lights, decorations, and even plastic cups instead of paper ones! It was a huge step up from the ninth-grade Sadie Hawkins dance I had gone to. Although I didn't technically go to the dance. I was on student council, so I stood outside by the back entrance and made sure nobody got raped.

Kelley and I walked into the party and took a big look around. It was pretty magical. Then right away a group of lesbians danced over to us in a tornado of pussy.

Lesbian Tornado: Hey, Kelley! Come dance with us!!!

Kelley: Maybe later!

Lesbian Tornado: Come on! We requested Evanescence!

Kelley: I do love Evanescence.

Me: Go ahead.

Kelley: Really?

Me: Ya. I can find someone to hang with for a while.

Kelley: Thanks! Save a dance for me?

Me: I'll save a dance. I probably won't save a cupcake, but a dance for sure.

Kelley: Deal.

And with that she was sucked up into the tornado of pussy

and I didn't see her till the end of the night. I looked around the room to see what I could do to fill my time. There was a dance circle that my friends were moshing in: no thank you. There was a photo booth with props and dumb hats: nightmare. There was a table filled with desserts and a chocolate fountain: thank God.

I made my way over and set up shop. As I was dunking my tenth Nutter Butter into the cascading waterfall of chocolate, I felt a tap on my shoulder. It was my teacher Mrs. Smith, and to say she was slightly intoxicated would be an understatement. From her breath and the fact that she was a grown woman forced to chaperone a prom on her night off, I'm going to assume she was alcohol-poisoning-level wasted. She was the kind of teacher who you knew wanted to be a rock star and teaching had been her fallback. I always enjoyed her class, mainly because she would let us sleep whenever she had a hangover.

Mrs. Smith: What are you doing over here?

Me: Raising my risk of type 2 diabetes.

Mrs. Smith: You don't already have that?

Me: I know, I'm an underachiever.

Mrs. Smith: You should be out there dancing!

Me: Me? Dance? I'd rather die while masturbating and be found by my mother.

Mrs. Smith: That was specific.

Me: I think about it a lot. Every time I masturbate I think, "This could be it. Maybe I should leave a note."

Mrs. Smith: You do realize I'm your teacher, right?

Me: You do realize you're drunk, right?

Mrs. Smith: Touché. So, where's your date?

Me: She ditched me to hang out with her lesbian friends.

Mrs. Smith: Wow. That's almost so sad it's hilarious.

Me: Ya. I'm hysterically laughing on the inside. I have to keep shoving Nutter Butters into my mouth to keep the laughter from coming out.

Mrs. Smith: You know, high school doesn't mean shit.

Me: Excuse me?

Mrs. Smith: Everyone thinks it's so important. Being popular, going on dates, getting voted prom king. None of it matters. After high school nobody gives a shit. You go to college as a total loser nobody, no matter how cool you were in high school. And then after you graduate college you're TOTALLY fucked.

Me: You make a lot of sense when you're drunk.

Mrs. Smith: Hey, ten years from now you're going to be cooler than any of these kids. Mark my words. You got something special.

Me: Thanks. Are you trying to have sex with me?

Mrs. Smith: No. Not yet. Maybe in ten years when you aren't a total loser.

Me: Understandable.

Mrs. Smith: Hey, you wanna dance?

Me: Isn't that like . . . highly inappropriate? Like Lifetime-movie inappropriate?

Mrs. Smith: Who cares! We only live once!

She took my hand and dragged me to the dance floor. The song changed to a slow jam, making the situation even more awkward, but she didn't care. She pulled me in close and led me like I was the girl. I had never danced with anyone before in my life and honestly, I was ok with her being my first. What's better than slow-dancing with your drunk teacher at your senior prom? Nothing. As the song ended the tornado of lesbians came around and dropped Kelley off.

Kelley: Can I cut in?

Mrs. Smith: Of course. I gotta go puke in the parking lot anyways.

Me: Stay classy, Mrs. Smith.

Now that I knew how to dance I grabbed Kelley's hand and led her through the last song of the night. It was pretty romantic, except for the whole "she's a lesbian and the thought of me having a penis makes her physically ill" part. We looked at each other and smiled. Yes, maybe it was weird to be going to the prom with your best friend, who had no interest in you whatsoever, but at least we were experiencing this together. And at least neither of us had gotten our period in our white dress. So fine, ok. Maybe it actually wasn't a total car crash of a prom. It was more of a fender bender with a few scratches and a lot of laughs.

ABOUT THE ARTIST

Jacqueline Colunga *is a young artist who resides in Lakewood, California. She has always been interested in art and spends her free time painting and drawing. She would love to make a career out of it.*

ACKNOWLEDGMENTS

I want to thank everyone in my life who has given me material for this book. I want to thank my family, who has loved me unconditionally and has always been BRUTALLY honest with me about my haircuts and fashion choices. You guys have given me enough material for ten books. I also want to thank my friends for sticking by my side even though I constantly chew food with my mouth open and always ask if your passive-aggressive tweets are about me. I want to thank my girlfriend, Lisa, for holding my hand in public and not making me walk ten steps behind her. I want to thank my audience, who has supported me since I uploaded my first video to my ShaneDawsonTV YouTube channel in 2008. Without you I would be nothing more than an insecure guy complaining about my life to just my family and friends. Now I have someone else to do that with. Thank you. And lastly, I want to thank God. Dude, you've got a sick sense of humor, but luckily so do I. Keep on filling my life with hilarious moments of awkwardness and embarrassment. I'd like this to be the first book of many. It can be like the Harry Potter franchise except instead of a story of a wizard conquering his demons it will be the story of a loser accepting them. Ya, that seems like a fun read!